THE MACMILLAN SHAKESPEARE

ADVISORY EDITOR: PHILIP BROCKBANK,
Professor of English and Director of the
Shakespeare Institute, University of Birmingham

GENERAL EDITOR: PETER HOLLINDALE,
Senior Lecturer in English and Education,
University of York

MACBETH

Other titles in the series

TWELFTH NIGHT edited by E. A. J. Honigmann
THE TEMPEST edited by A. C. and J. E. Spearing
A MIDSUMMER NIGHT'S DREAM
edited by Norman Sanders
HAMLET edited by Nigel Alexander
JULIUS CAESAR edited by D. R. Elloway
ROMEO AND JULIET edited by J. C. Gibson
AS YOU LIKE IT edited by Peter Hollindale
RICHARD III edited by Richard Adams
THE TAMING OF THE SHREW edited by R. C. Hood
HENRY V edited by Brian Phythian
THE MERCHANT OF VENICE
edited by Christopher Parry
KING LEAR edited by Philip Edwards
RICHARD II edited by Richard Adams
HENRY IV, PART 1 edited by Peter Hollindale
MUCH ADO ABOUT NOTHING edited by Jan McKeith
THE WINTER'S TALE edited by Christopher Parry
HENRY IV, PART 2 edited by Tony Parr
OTHELLO edited by Celia Hilton and
R. T. Jones
ANTONY AND CLEOPATRA edited by Jan McKeith
and Richard Adams
CORIOLANUS edited by Tony Parr

THE MACMILLAN SHAKESPEARE

MACBETH

Edited by

D. R. Elloway

Macmillan Education

First published 1971
Reprinted 1972, 1974, 1976, 1977, 1978 (twice), 1980 (twice), 1981, 1982, 1983, 1984, 1985 (twice)

Published by
MACMILLAN EDUCATION LTD
Houndmills, Basingstoke, Hampshire RG21 2XS
and London
Companies and representatives
throughout the world

Printed in Great Britain by
Anchor Brendon Ltd
Tiptree, Essex

ISBN 0–333–13571–7

CONTENTS

PREFACE

All editions of *Macbeth* must be based on the text as it was first published in the 1623 collected edition of Shakespeare's plays, known as the First Folio. Some of the more generally accepted emendations suggested by later editors have been accepted for this edition, and the more important of these are referred to in the notes. The spelling and punctuation have been modernised, but something of the weight of the original punctuation has been retained.

The editor is deeply indebted to the many previous interpreters and editors of the play, in particular to Professor Kenneth Muir for his edition of *Macbeth* in the Arden Shakespeare.

D.R.E.

INTRODUCTION

I: *THE PLAY IN 1606*

Macbeth was one of the most topical of Shakespeare's plays when it was first produced. It was written in the first half of 1606, shortly after the discovery of the Gunpowder Plot, when – like Scotland after the murder of Duncan – the country was still shaken by the 'fears and scruples' aroused by this nearly successful attempt to murder the King, his heirs, and most of the nobility. Ross's description of the troubled state of Scotland

> when we hold rumour
> From what we fear, yet know not what we fear,
> But float upon a wild and violent sea
> Each way, and move –

must have reflected the perturbation in England at the end of 1605.

It is the echoes of the Plot that fix the date of the play with greatest certainty. The medallion struck to commemorate its discovery is recalled in one of Lady Macbeth's speeches (see I. 5.64–5 and note), and there can be little doubt that the Porter's references to equivocation allude to the trial on 28 March of Henry Garnet, Provincial of the English Jesuits, for complicity in the Plot. Garnet had persistently denied any knowledge of it, and when he was finally compelled to admit his guilt he excused his previous false denials as 'equivocation', maintaining that this was justifiable, and might even be confirmed by oath and sacrament, in a righteous cause. Perjury was not perjury if, as the Porter puts it, it was 'for God's sake'. Equivocation became the fashionable topic of the day, the subject for serious treatises and grim jokes. When the Porter comments that his equivocator 'could not equivocate to heaven' he is echoing the sardonic remarks current at the time, such as Dudley Carleton's prediction that Garnet would 'be hanged without equivocation', or Garnet's own words on the scaffold – 'It is no time now to equivocate'.

Moreover, as Dr Leslie Hotson[1] has pointed out, two of the conspirators, Catesby and Winters, were natives of Shakespeare's Warwickshire, and one of the centres of the Plot was Clopton House, near Stratford. Sir Everard Digby had collected a party of Catholic gentry there to seize the Princess Elizabeth, and the other conspirators fled there after the arrest of Fawkes, and were nearly captured by the bailiff of Stratford. In London they seem to have frequented the Mermaid tavern, traditionally the social centre for Shakespeare and his fellow dramatists; Ben Jonson dined there with Catesby a few days before the Plot was discovered. Shakespeare may thus have had a personal interest in the conspiracy, although there is no evidence that he was acquainted with any of the conspirators.

Even without this, however, he must have been powerfully affected by the discovery of the holocaust that they had planned – 'their diabolicall Domesday', as James I called it. Macduff describes the murder of Duncan in the same terms when he likens it to 'the great doom's image', and his horrified outburst was not merely conventional exaggeration. Regicide was regarded with peculiar horror at the time. The King was God's regent on earth, the 'Lord's anointed temple' (II. 3. 67) in which divinity resided. The sanctity of kingship and the piety of a true king are constantly stressed in the play (see III. 6. 27, 45–7, IV. 3. 108–11, 140–59, 238–9, V. 9. 38). Thus the murder of the king was not only treason, but sacrilege. It was the supreme violation of the moral order of the universe that had been ordained by God, and was evident throughout His creation. The ordered hierarchy of social ranks in the state was seen as a reflection of the universal hierarchy of being that ascended from inanimate matter through vegetable and animal life to man, and thence

[1] *I, William Shakespeare* (London, 1937).

through the spiritual orders to God, at its apex. As the universe was sustained by God, so the well-being of the kingdom depended on the person of the king. An active 'correspondence' was thought to exist between these two orders: disturbances in the heavens foretold disorders in the state, and disorder in the political realm produced similar convulsions in the natural. When Duncan is murdered, the sun – the monarch of the heavens – is darkened, the kingly falcon is killed by a mousing owl, and Duncan's horses make war against their natural superior, man –

'Tis unnatural,
Even like the deed that's done. (II. 4. 10–11)

A similar correspondence was thought to exist between the human constitution and that of the state. Man was a 'little kingdom' in which the hierarchy of the faculties resembled that of the different ranks in society: reason ruled over the will, which in turn controlled the appetites and desires. Physical and psychological health depended on the preservation of this order, and both would be disturbed if a particular desire was allowed to become too powerful and to rebel against the dictates of reason. Disease in the body and mind corresponded to insurrection in the kingdom, and because of the close relationship between this psychological order and that of society the health of the kingdom depended on the moral health of its monarch. Macbeth and Lady Macbeth allow their desire for the throne to overcome their rational and spiritual insight, and the consequent disorder in their personalities is reflected in the chaotic state of Scotland. Both the tyrant and his realm are diseased; Macbeth wishes that the Doctor who is attending Lady Macbeth could 'cast the water' of his land,

find her disease,
And purge it to a sound and pristine health, (V. 3. 50–2)

but he is himself the disease that must be purged by the blood of the loyal thanes (V. 2. 28–9, and see also IV. 3. 214–15). Conversely, the true heir to the throne is 'the medicine of the sickly weal' (V. 2. 27). The clearest evidence of the spiritual authority of kingship was the miraculous healing power of the king, which was still believed in literally. As late as the eighteenth century it was thought that he could cure scrofula – the 'king's evil' – by touching those afflicted with it, a power that was supposed to have been bestowed on the saintly Edward the Confessor and passed on to his royal descendents (see IV. 3. 140–59).

The necessity for order in the kingdom was a common theme for Shakespeare, but in no other play – not even in *Richard II* – does he uphold the divine authority of the king as unequivocally as he does in *Macbeth*. This would have been very gratifying to James I. Coming from Scotland, he was anxious to demonstrate his right to the English throne, and it was to show that he was the legitimate king that he resumed the practice of touching for scrofula, although his Calvinist upbringing inclined him to regard it as a relic of Catholic superstition. Thus he would have appreciated Shakespeare's account of the ceremony at the English court; indeed, the whole of that scene would have appealed to him, with its catalogue of the vices of tyranny and the corresponding 'king-becoming graces'. He fancied himself as a 'philosopher king', and in his *Basilikon Doron* (1599) had compiled a similar list of royal virtues for the instruction of his eldest son, contrasting them with the tyranny of a usurper, who – like Macbeth – lives in continual fear and is lawfully killed by his own subjects. Shakespeare certainly aimed to please James with *Macbeth*, and one of its first performances was probably at Hampton Court in August, 1606, to entertain the King and his brother-in-law, Christian IV of Denmark. The play may have been written especially for this state visit.

II: *THE WITCHES*

The prominence of the witches in the play would have been equally appropriate for this occasion, as it was when he was returning from Denmark after his marriage to Christian's sister, Anne, that James had first come into contact with witchcraft. A coven of witches in North Berwickshire had tried to practise the black arts against him, and the confession of one of them, Agnes Seaton, was published in a pamphlet entitled *News from Scotland* in 1591. She had first hung up a toad 'by the heels' and caught the venom that dropped from it (compare IV. 1. 6–8) so that she could use it to anoint an article of clothing that the King had worn. Being unable to obtain any of his soiled linen, she and her colleagues had christened a cat, tied to it parts of the body of a dead man (compare IV. 1. 26, 29) and carried it out to sea before the town of Leith, 'sailing in their riddles or sieves' (compare I. 3. 8). The storm that they raised by this means hindered the King's return and wrecked a ship carrying gifts for the new Queen. James at first doubted this story, but agreed that the winds had been strangely contrary to his own ship, and he was finally convinced when Agnes Seaton told him the very words that had passed between him and Anne on their wedding night. The subject fascinated him: 'In respect of the strangeness of these matters' he 'took great delight to be present at their examinations', and he was doubtless gratified by their explanation of the devil's special hatred for him – 'by reason the King is the greatest enemy he hath in the world'. His interest led him to write a treatise on witchcraft, *Demonology* (1597, published in England 1603).

James's initial scepticism was not so uncommon at the time; the best known account of the beliefs current about witches – Reginald Scot's *Discovery of Witchcraft* (1584) – was written to expose them as superstitions. But most of Shakespeare's contemporaries would have had no doubts about their truth. Murder by witchcraft had been punishable by death since 1563, and a new act in 1604 made any practice of it a capital offence. Whatever his private opinions, Shakespeare certainly accepted the reality of witches for the purpose of his play.

Some doubts about the nature of the witches in *Macbeth* have been aroused by the fact that they are called the 'Weird Sisters', a phrase that Shakespeare borrowed from Holinshed's *Chronicles of England, Scotland and Ireland* (1577) – his source for the story of the play. In Holinshed 'weird' retains its older meaning of 'fate' (it was originally a noun) – they are referred to as 'the weird sisters, that is . . . the goddesses of destinie'. But Shakespeare may well not have known this meaning of the word, which survived only in the North, and, as A. C. Bradley[1] pointed out, the activities described by the witches at the beginning of I. iii. are characteristic of the traditional witches of popular belief, rather than of goddesses of destiny. They are not, it is true, the harmless old women who suffered in the witch trials, but rather how their persecutors thought of them, and how they were sometimes deluded into thinking of themselves.

In all respects they conform to the popular theories of witchcraft at the times. They have no power of their own, but gain it by selling their souls to the devil. They are only the 'instruments' of darkness (I. 3. 124); Shakespeare's witches refer even to the apparitions that they raise as their 'masters' (IV. 1. 63). According to Scot, it was believed that the devil taught them to steal unbaptized children (compare IV. 1. 30–1)

> and seethe them in a cauldron, until their flesh be made potable. Of the thickest whereof they make ointments (compare IV. 1. 32), whereby they ride in the air (compare IV. 1. 138)

and James records in *Demonology* that the devil

[1] *Shakespearean Tragedy* (London, 1904).

> causeth them to joint dead corpses (compare I. 3. 28, IV. 1. 29), and to make powders thereof (compare IV. 1. 23 and note), mixing such other things there amongst, as he gives unto them.

The 'familiar spirits' who both controlled and assisted the witch were minor devils who often took the form of animals – Scot mentions in particular toads and cats (compare I. 1. 8, 9). With their aid witches could 'foreshow things to come' and 'raise hail, tempests, and hurtfull weather' (compare I. 1. 2, 3. 11–25, IV. 1. 52–60). One detail that Shakespeare may have borrowed directly from the *Demonology* is the 'fog and filthy air' into which the witches vanish at the end of the first scene – James had attempted to explain their invisibility by suggesting that the devil might 'thicken and obscure so the air . . . that the beams of any other man's eyes cannot pierce through the same, to see them'.

III: *THE SOURCES*

The choice of the subject of the play from Holinshed's *Chronicles* must also have been intended to please the King. Shakespeare may even have been in Oxford in August 1605 when James was welcomed there by three scholars representing sibyls, who complimented him by recalling the promises made by the Weird Sisters to his ancestor, Banquo. He was very proud of his descent from an unbroken line of eight monarchs, springing from the marriage of Walter Steward (or Stuart), a descendent of Banquo, to Marjory, daughter of Robert the Bruce and a descendent of Duncan. His ancestry is duly celebrated by the show of eight kings, with the 'twofold balls and treble sceptres' prophesying the unions of the English and Scottish thrones under James. H. N. Paul[1] has suggested that Shakespeare may also have known John Leslie's *De Origine, Moribus, et Rebus Gestis Scotorum*, in which the

[1] *The Royal Play of 'Macbeth'* (New York, 1950).

family tree of the Stuarts is represented as an actual tree, with the name of Banquo at the root (compare III. 1. 5–6, IV. 1. 86 s.d.), and the repeated emphasis on the fertility of Banquo's line might have implied a flattering comparison with the sterility of the Tudors, which had enabled James to succeed them. To be sure, neither Banquo nor Duncan is particularly admirable as the story is told by Holinshed. Banquo knows of Macbeth's plot against the King, while Duncan is described as 'a dull coward and slouthfull person'. Macbeth compares favourably with him at the beginning of his reign—

> he set his whole intention to mainteine justice, and to punish all enormities and abuses, which had chanced through the feeble and slouthfull administration of Duncane.

Moreover, Holinshed supplies Macbeth with an excuse for killing Duncan. According to old Scottish law, the throne should have passed to him, as next in blood to the King, if Duncan had died before his eldest son came of age. By creating Malcolm Prince of Cumberland – and so heir apparent – while he was still a minor, Duncan was attempting to deprive Macbeth of his right to the succession – a circumstance that Shakespeare ignores. But he was writing a tragedy, not a history, and other descriptions of Duncan that he may have known, such as that in John Skene's 'Table of all the Kings of Scotland' (1603), were much more complimentary to the King.

Other parts of the *Chronicles* may also have contributed to the play. The character of Lady Macbeth is almost entirely Shakespeare's addition – Holinshed only mentions in passing that Macbeth was encouraged by his wife – but the enlargement of her part may have been suggested by his account of another royal murder, that of King Duff by Donwald, captain of the castle of Forres. Donwald's wife not only encouraged him, 'though he abhorred the act greatlie in heart', but also 'shewed him the meanes whereby he might soonest accomplish it' (compare I. 7. 61–72). Many of the other circumstances of this murder appear in the early scenes of *Macbeth*: the King's great trust for Donwald, which betrays him into lodging unguarded at Forres; the banquet which reduces the servants to drunken stupor; 'the bed all beraied with bloud'; Donwald's pretence of horrified innocence when the murder is discovered; his slaying of the two chamberlains 'as guiltie of that heinous murder', and the supernatural manifestations that accompanied it (see II. 3. 53–60; 4. 1–18 and note).

The two episodes in which Shakespeare follows his source most closely are those which Holinshed treats with most detail – Macbeth's first meeting with the witches and the testing of Macduff by Malcolm. The latter episode in the play is almost a versified synopsis of Holinshed's lengthy account, while for the former Shakespeare took not only the prophecies and the immediate fulfilment of one of them, but also such dramatic detail as Banquo's intervention after the witches have saluted Macbeth and his light-hearted scepticism about their predictions. According to Holinshed, Macbeth at first adopted the same attitude –

> This was reputed at the first but some vaine fantasticall illusion by Mackbeth and Banquho, insomuch that Banquho would call Mackbeth in jest, king of Scotland; and Mackbeth againe would call him in sport likewise, the father of manie kings.

By distinguishing their reactions Shakespeare gives us an immediate insight into the difference between their characters.

For the most part, however, Shakespeare radically condenses and simplifies Holinshed's narrative. The *Chronicles* describe in detail the three campaigns of Macbeth and Banquo against Macdonwald, Sweno, and a Danish army sent by Canute; in *Macbeth* the first two are only reported, and the third omitted altogether, perhaps in deference to Christian of Denmark. The historical Macbeth reigned for seventeen years, with ten years of just rule before the murder of Banquo; in the play this period seems to be reduced to at most a few months – the murder of Banquo follows soon after that of Duncan, and the seven years of tyranny are represented economically by the murder of Lady Macduff and her son, with the speeches of Ross, Lennox and Macduff to suggest the general reign of terror. Time is always elastic in Shakespeare's tragedies. One is vaguely aware that a considerable period must have elapsed for Macbeth to have such a grip on the country, yet from the actual indications in the text only a few weeks could have passed between the beginning of the play and Macduff's flight to England.

IV: *THE STRUCTURE*

This telescoping of time makes *Macbeth* the most concentrated of all Shakespeare's plays, and the additions and alterations that he made to Holinshed's account increase the concentration, giving the play a closely interwoven pattern. In the *Chronicles*, for example, Macbeth is warned to beware of Macduff by 'certeine wizzards', while the reassurances that he would not be killed by man born of woman or until Birnam Wood comes to Dunsinane are attributed to 'a certeine witch'. By giving all three prophecies to apparitions raised by the same Weird Sisters who originally accosted Macbeth Shakespeare greatly increases the symmetry of the action. The cauldron scene, for which there is no hint in Holinshed, balances the first meeting with the witches, and the prophecies in each follow the same pattern – three statements directly related to Macbeth, followed by a prediction of the fertility of Banquo's line that sours the earlier promises. The first movement of the play is activated by the first set of prophecies; then the witches recharge Macbeth for the second movement, with an ironic combination of hopes and fears that leads to his downfall.

If the two movements of the play are given a formal relationship to each other by the witch scenes, the hinge on which the action turns is the banquet scene, which was another addition by Shakespeare – in Holinshed Banquo is murdered after the banquet. It is the turning point of the plot: while it represents the culmination of Macbeth's ambition – it is the only time that we see him as King, regally entertaining his thanes – it is also the occasion on which he first gives himself away to Lennox and the other lords. The murder of Banquo ties the two parts of the play tightly together: it should have removed the only threat to Macbeth that remained in Scotland, but it is this murder that forces him to disclose his guilt. The irony is concentrated in his injunction to Banquo that he should 'Fail not our feast' (III. 1. 27) – so that he should be murdered; Banquo doesn't fail it, with disastrous consequences for the murderer. The scene is equally a pivot for the characters. It is the last occasion on which Lady Macbeth takes control of the situation, but already she is withdrawn – she 'keeps her state' – in anticipation of her collapse at the end of the play. Similarly, it is the last time that Macbeth loses his nerve, but on this occasion he is able to master his terror and dismiss the ghost himself. After that he can look at his fears objectively (III. 4. 141–2), and at the end of the scene he displays a new ruthlessness – 'For mine own good/All causes shall give way'. His first meeting with the witches had been apparently accidental – while embracing evil he had tried to avoid recognising the nature of his action – but now he deliberately seeks them out and commits himself to evil with open eyes

> now I am bent to know
> By the worst means the worst.

He himself recognises that this is the turning point – or the point of no return:

> I am in blood
> Stepped in so far that, should I wade no more,
> Returning were as tedious as go o'er.

The situation develops with extraordinary rapidity. At the beginning of the banquet Macbeth is still the newly-crowned King, rather self-consciously ingratiating himself with his thanes; by the end he is a hardened tyrant, with a 'servant fee'd' in every house. Ten years of psychological development have been compressed into a single scene.

This tight structure gives the play much of the symbolic force of a mediaeval morality play, such as was still being performed in Shakespeare's day. In these plays moral problems were dramatised directly; their characters were personifications of abstract virtues and vices, or supernatural beings – angels or devils – who stated the moral issues explicitly. The hero, for whose soul these abstract forces contested, was a generalised representation of humanity – 'Everyman', in the best known of the moralities. The witches in *Macbeth* perform something of the same function as the morality devils, although in a more subtle way, and the play focuses on the moral issues by omitting irrelevant historical detail, but the characters are certainly not generalised abstractions. Instead, the universal relevance of the action, which the moralities conveyed by the use of such characters, is suggested in *Macbeth* by its compressed, formal structure. We watch not an accidental sequence of events, but a pattern of moral cause and effect, of sin and retribution, which is seen to be fundamental to many different circumstances. The sense of inevitability comes from the speed of the play, the immediacy with which an action is followed by its consequence, and from the interrelation of its events. The murder of Banquo which was meant to ensure Macbeth's safety immediately destroys it, and Macbeth's success in seeking reassurance from the witches actually contributes to his destruction because of his excessive reliance on their promises: 'security', as Hecate says (III. 5. 32–3), is the cause of his insecurity.

The morality character of the play is further increased by the number of brief general statements uttered by characters who appear to be standing apart from the action and commenting on its significance – such as Banquo's warning about the 'instruments of darkness' (I. 3. 122–6) or the Doctor's comment on 'unnatural deeds' (V. 1. 72–76). When the speaker himself is not aware of the full significance of what he is saying the force of these statements is increased by dramatic irony – irony that arises when the words imply a further, and more important, meaning, which only the audience can recognise. Thus when the treachery of Cawdor prompts Duncan to the general reflection that

> There's no art
> To find the mind's construction in the face (I. 4. 11–12)

the immediate entry of Macbeth reminds us that these words are even more relevant to him. The general truth of the statement is underlined as Duncan goes on to display an equally 'absolute trust' in the man whom, ironically, he has just created the new Thane of Cawdor, and to assure him that 'More is thy due than more than all can pay', while Macbeth is already plotting to take 'all' for himself.

A similar purpose is served by the short, choric scenes in which the characters comment externally on the action of the play like the chorus in a Greek tragedy. In II. 4. Ross and the Old Man relate the murder of Duncan to the universal pattern of order by describing its repercussions in the natural world, and in III. 6. Lennox delivers an ironically detached commentary on Macbeth's behaviour and the Lord contrasts his tyranny with the 'faithful homage' and 'free honours' enjoyed under a 'holy King'.

The witch scenes and the catalogue of royal virtues and vices in IV. iii. similarly define the moral poles between which the action of the play moves; indeed, there is not an episode that does not contribute, if less explicitly, to this generalising commentary on the particular events taking place. The play continually modulates out of the immediate situation to suggest by an image or an ironic play on words the universal significance of the action.

The most striking example of this is the drunken rambling of the Porter. Its themes might seem to have been included merely for their topical interest, but they are by no means incidental to the play. Equivocation is at the heart of its evil. The witches equivocate with Macbeth in order to destroy him with half-truths (see V. 5. 42–4, 8. 19–22, and p 26), and Macbeth equivocates with his conscience in order to bring himself to commit murder. He tries to persuade himself that he can ignore its spiritual consequences and 'jump the life to come', but the Porter is there to remind us that the equivocator could not 'equivocate to heaven'. The topical relevance of this speech only increases its general significance, bridging the five centuries between the murder of Duncan and the Gunpowder Plot.

Moreover, Kenneth Muir[1] has pointed out that the Porter's bawdy discourse about the effects of drunkenness on lechery – 'it provokes the desire, but it takes away the performance' (II. 3. 28–9) – is a burlesque commentary on the similar conflict between desire and performance within Macbeth (see I, 4. 52–3, 5. 21–4, 7. 39–41). Drink 'equivocates' with the drunkard just as the witches equivocate with Macbeth. Both raise deceitful hopes of enjoyment, hopes that are disappointed for the drunkard by the very intoxication that excited them, and for Macbeth by the means he uses to satisfy his ambition, and that afterwards destroy his peace of mind and enjoyment of power. The Porter is continuing on a different level that

[1] Introduction to the Arden edition of *Macbeth* (London, 1951).

examination of the nature of manhood that Macbeth initiated when he protested to Lady Macbeth that it is not manly to dare do more than 'may become a man' (see I. 7. 46–7, III. 1. 90–100 and notes). The drunkard thinks he is 'more the man' (I. 7. 51), only to find that intoxication has destroyed his virility. Evil is seen to have the same basic character in murder as in drunken lechery. Both Macbeth and the drunkard are deceived by

> Vaulting ambition, which o'erleaps itself,
> And falls on the other (I. 7. 27–8)

– a literal fall ('giving him the lie' – II. 3. 35) in the case of the latter. All the Porter's imaginary guests have made the same error: the farmer was not content with a moderate profit, the tailor tried to be too cunning in the theft of cloth, and the equivocator thought he could equivocate to heaven. Nothing could be more inappropriate than to describe the Porter's speeches as 'comic relief' – put in to please the groundlings; his devil-portering is a macabre epilogue to the murder of Duncan, pointing out where we have been during the previous scene – in hell, for hell is a state of mind that one creates for oneself. Shakespeare's own audience was much less likely to miss its moral purpose, for, as Muir also points out, the Porter of Hell Gate was a traditional comic character in the Morality plays.

With the events of the play thus loaded with significance the dramatic action itself is cut to the bone. Shakespeare highlights the relevant events and allows the rest to slip into obscurity. Characters such as Ross and Lennox are introduced to contribute their threads to the total pattern, and we know – and need to know – no more of them. Lennox is a particularly confusing character. In III. 6. he is rehearsing Macbeth's crimes and praying for the success of Macduff's mission to England, yet at the end of the next scene he is loyally reporting Macduff's flight to Macbeth, as if it were news that had just been brought to him. The suggestion that these two scenes have been reversed (see introductory note to III. 6.) does not solve this problem as Lennox would then know of Macduff's flight before he is told by the Lord. It seems that Shakespeare was not in the least interested in Lennox as a character, but used him for two quite different functions – or even that the two are supposed to be performed by different characters, but that both parts were played by the same actor.

Questions affecting more important characters are also left open. We are not told, for example, why Macbeth sent a third murderer to help despatch Banquo, nor why Macduff risked leaving his family unguarded. But both these actions are prepared for – Macbeth's self-justification and anxious questioning of the murderers in III. i. show how uneasy he is about trusting them with the murder, and we know that he is planning some action against Macduff. The very uncertainty about their motives contributes to the atmosphere of uneasy suspicion that is engendered by tyranny. The audience is placed in the same situation as the characters, aware of dark plotting that it does not fully understand. Our doubts about the wisdom of Macduff's hasty departure are shared by Lady Macduff and by Malcolm (IV. 3. 25–8), and add to our sense of the moral chaos in Scotland, when even men who are 'noble, wise, judicious' are placed in impossible dilemmas and must risk making the wrong decision rather than not make any decision at all.

We are also left in the dark about the nature of Macbeth's earlier plotting against Duncan, which Lady Macbeth charges him with (I. 7. 47–54). His guilty start when he hears the witches' prophecies also suggests that he had already thought of killing the King; they say nothing of murder – in fact, as Macbeth says himself (I. 3. 143–4), the knowledge that he was fated to become king might have persuaded him that he no longer needed to kill Duncan. Yet his thoughts fly immediately to murder, although his horrified response hardly suggests the practical determination that Lady Macbeth later attributes to him –

Nor time, nor place,
Did then adhere, and yet you would make both.

This has led Dover Wilson[1] to suggest that there was originally a scene following I. 3, in which Macbeth 'broke the enterprise' to his wife, and that this was omitted when the play was revised for performance at court – James liked plays to be short. It is doubtful, however, if anything would be gained by making the nature of this plotting more explicit. It is sufficient that we should know that Macbeth had contemplated murder before meeting the witches, and by the time we reach I. 7. our primary interest is in the means by which Lady Macbeth persuades him to go through with it. She may well be exaggerating the degree to which he was previously committed to the deed, and even if we believe her we are not going to have time in a theatre to speculate on when this earlier discussion could have taken place.

A more serious problem is raised by Banquo's failure to take any action against Macbeth, even though he is virtually certain of his guilt (III. 1. 2–3). From their first appearance the characters of the two seem to be deliberately contrasted. The openness of a clear conscience that was evident in Banquo's light-hearted response to the witches is equally apparent in his readiness to admit that he is troubled by their prophecies, while Macbeth guiltily pretends to ignore them (II. 1. 20–1), and in the disingenuousness of his replies to Macbeth's questions about his movements before the banquet. There is a singular frankness – a 'clarity' – about his character; when sounded by Macbeth he insists that he must keep his 'bosom *franchised* and allegiance *clear*' (II. 1. 28). It is felt especially in the lyrical quality and limpid atmosphere of his 'martlet' speech (I. 6. 3–10); the delicacy of the air – 'heaven's breath' – contrasts directly with the 'thick night' and 'dunnest smoke of hell' invoked by Macbeth and his wife

[1] Introduction to the New Shakespeare edition of *Macbeth* (Cambridge, 1947).

(I. 5. 49–50, III. 2. 50), as the 'temple-haunting' martlets – symbols of fertility – contrast with their 'murd'ring ministers' and 'night's black agents'. Banquo has a genuine 'royalty of nature', before which the usurper is abashed; in contrast to the disorder in Macbeth's character, his faculties are serenely balanced –

> And, to that dauntless temper of his mind,
> He hath a wisdom that doth guide his valour
> To act in safety. (III, 1. 48–56)

Yet in spite of his pious resolution after Duncan's murder (II. 3. 128–30) he does nothing to expose the murderer. It may be significant that his thoughts pass directly from his suspicion of Macbeth to his hope for his own posterity; this seems to weigh with him more than Macbeth's guilt. The 'cursed thoughts' from which he is suffering in II. 1. show that even he is not impervious to the suggestions of witches; he too has bad dreams. It could be that his preoccupation with the fortunes of his own family deflects him from his responsibility to the state. Ironically, it is his ghost – real or imagined – that performs the duty that Banquo failed in while alive.

V: *THE TRAGIC HERO*

One does not feel the personality of any of the other supporting characters as one does that of Banquo, yet even he is less developed than the second-rank characters in many of Shakespeare's other plays; one may deduce the conflict that is going on inside him after the murder of Duncan, but one does not see him wrestling with his conscience as one does Claudius in *Hamlet*. The whole weight of the play rests on the characters of the two protagonists, Macbeth and Lady Macbeth.

It is here that Shakespeare's compression of his historical source might have had its most serious effect. With Macbeth's reign reduced to a short period of unrelieved tyranny and his earlier patriotic deeds merely reported at the beginning of the play, one might be tempted to see his death not as the tragic fall of a hero but as just retribution on a villain – to accept Malcom's dismissal of him as 'this dead butcher' (V. 9. 35). For the play to be a tragedy the audience must be able to identify with the hero and sympathise with him in his fall – to say, instead, with the Doctor, 'God, God forgive us all' (V. 1. 76).

Macbeth is certainly the most 'villainous' of Shakespeare's tragic heroes. His courage in defence of Scotland is emphasised in the opening scenes, yet even this is of a singularly brutal kind – it is perhaps when he 'unseams' Macdonwald that he appears most like a 'butcher'. Yet we do sympathise with him. While depriving him of many of the virtues possessed by the historical Macbeth, Shakespeare substitutes an imaginative penetration into his character which compels us to sympathise – to 'feel with' him, which is what 'sympathy' means. There is no doubt of his humanity, even when he commits 'inhuman' crimes. We live with him; in the scenes before and immediately after Duncan's murder we are immured not only in Macbeth's castle, surrounded by the darkness and the creatures of the night that inhabit his and his wife's imaginations, but within his mind, sharing his moral conflict and imprisoned in the mental world created by his hallucinations. These scenes are peculiarly claustrophobic, which is why the knocking on the gate after the murder has such an impact, as the outside world breaks in on this guilty isolation. De Quincey described it in his classic essay 'On the Knocking at the Gate in *Macbeth*':

> when the deed is done, when the work of darkness is perfect, then the world of darkness passes away like a pageantry in the clouds: the knocking at the gate is heard; and it makes known audibly that the reaction has commenced; the human has made its reflux upon the fiendish; the pulses of life are beginning to beat again; and the re-establishment of the goings-on of the world

> in which we live, first makes us profoundly sensible of the awful parenthesis that had suspended them.

We are made aware of just how closely we have been identifying with Macbeth.

We not only see through his eyes, but are taken into those parts of his mind that he desperately tries to conceal from himself. When he first thinks of murder there is no doubt of the horror with which he regards it; in his soliloquy (I. 3. 130–42) he refers to it only obliquely as if he cannot bear to look at it directly. He tries to consider the situation in practical terms – 'If chance will have me king, why, chance may crown me' – and to prevaricate – 'We will speak further' (I. 5. 70) – but his moral awareness continually finds expression in the images that are forced up from the less conscious levels of his mind. As he soliloquises at the beginning of I. 7. he purports to be weighing up the chances of success in a hard-headed manner, considering whether he can get away with it

> here,
> But here, upon this bank and shoal of time,

but the implications of the very metaphors he uses expose the superficiality of such calculations. 'Time' – temporal life – is only a 'bank and shoal' that will soon be swallowed up in the ocean of eternity – 'the life to come', that Macbeth pretends he can shrug off. The whole speech moves on these two levels. He refers to Duncan's virtues and his own obligations to the King ostensibly as reasons for supposing that the murder must be revenged, because of the horror it will excite, but the apocalyptic imagery of pity as

> a naked new-born babe,
> Striding the blast, or heaven's cherubin, horsed
> Upon the sightless couriers of the air

shows that he is equally moved by the horror himself. It is this that persuades him not to murder Duncan, although he pretends to reach his decision on merely practical grounds.

This conflict between the explicit statement and the imagery through which it is expressed mirrors the conflict in Macbeth's mind. He suffers from a sort of schizophrenia as he tries to repress the moral side of his nature. The unity of his personality, his 'single state of man', was already shaken when he heard the prophecies of the witches, and from that moment he is torn by the contradictory impulses which his wife analyses so precisely in her first soliloquy – he would not play false, and yet would wrongly win. He can commit murder only by shutting his eyes to the real nature of the deed; he must let 'the eye wink at the hand' (I. 4. 52), as if the hand were acting mechanically without his being aware of its action.

Lady Macbeth exploits this when she persuades him to the murder. She keeps the argument on the practical level, showing him how easy will be the course of action that she will arrange, and insisting that he is already committed to it and has only to be carried along by events. But the tension in both of them is evident in her own taut image, 'But screw your courage to the sticking-place' – any tighter, one feels, and it would snap – and in Macbeth's tremendous effort to

> bend up
> Each corporal agent to this terrible feat. (I. 7. 60, 79–80)

He must manipulate his corporeal faculties as if they were detached from himself. That is how he goes to murder Duncan, commenting on his own actions as if they were performed by another person. It is he who is 'withered Murder', and 'Tarquin's ravishing strides' are his strides, as he moves 'like a ghost' toward his design (II. 2. 52–6).

After the murder his disintegration is complete. Neither his physical nor his moral being seems his own. He regards his hands as if they no longer belong to him – 'What hands are here? Ha! they pluck out mine eyes' – and the moral sense that he has disowned is projected out of his own mind into the hallucinations that he is forced to dwell on compulsively. 'To know my deed, 'twere best not know myself', he cries, and while the horror is on him he no longer does 'know himself'. By the last act of the play

> all that is within him does condemn
> Itself for being there. (V. 2. 24–5)

This is not merely the isolated experience of one particular murderer. Macbeth's identification of himself as 'withered Murder' – which sounds like one of the personified characters in a morality play – points to its general relevance, and the experience of his wife may be seen to follow a similar pattern, even though her fears are much more firmly controlled. There is a marked parallel between their invocations to night to hide the murder both from heaven and from themselves (see I. 4. 50–3, I. 5. 49–53, and also III. 2. 46–53); she too must 'stop up th' access and passage to remorse'. Apart from a single touch of human feeling (II. 2. 12–13) she seems completely ruthless, but as he becomes more hardened, she weakens, and when her nerve finally cracks her conscience asserts itself in forms that are identical with the hallucinations that tormented him after the murder of Duncan. Now it is she who believes that her hands will never be cleansed of blood – 'all the perfumes of Arabia' exactly parallels Macbeth's 'all great Neptune's ocean' – and the voice that Macbeth heard crying 'Sleep no more!' was also foretelling her inability to find rest in sleep. Previously she had summoned darkness, now she has a light by her continually (V. 1. 22–3). Because her moral scruples were more sternly repressed their power over her is all the greater. In her sleep-walking she is reduced to the same hypnotic condition as Macbeth when he went to murder Duncan, but unlike him she cannot recover from it.

VI: *THE SUPERNATURAL*

This study of evil is further generalised by the way in which it is interwoven with the supernatural structure of the play. It has been suggested that the trance-like state of Macbeth and Lady Macbeth, and Macbeth's 'raptness' when the witches first tempt him and he sees Banquo's ghost, would have indicated to a Jacobean audience that they were the victims of demonic possession. They behave compulsively, as if they were controlled by evil spirits rather than by their own conscious minds. Macbeth's inability to pray (II. 2. 28–33) is another symptom of this condition, and Lady Macbeth's 'damned spot' might have suggested the devil's mark that was to be found on a witch. She actually assumes the role of a witch when she summons the 'spirits that tend on mortal thoughts' to possess her body (see I. 5. 39–49 and notes), and the Doctor's comment that she needs the divine more than the physician might mean that she is in need of exorcism as well as spiritual healing. 'Fiendlike' certainly seems a more apt description of her than 'butcher' does of Macbeth.

But Shakespeare is not merely portraying demonic possession. The Jacobeans were less simple-minded about the supernatural than is often supposed; their psychological theory may have been rudimentary, but their psychological observation was as acute as ours. The sleepwalking is at least as true to twentieth-century theories of repression as it is to seventeenth-century beliefs in possession; the 'spot' that brands Lady Macbeth is, after all, in her mind, not on her body. For Shakespeare and his audience supernatural forces were not only external powers, but forces within the mind. Evil spirits could have no influence over human beings unless they had already admitted evil into their minds, just as in the play it appears that Macbeth has already entertained the murderous thoughts in which the witches encourage him. If he and his wife are possessed by evil, it is because they allow themselves to be possessed; the compulsion is psychological rather than supernatural.

A sharp distinction between these two elements in the play misrepresents it, for in *Macbeth* the one continually merges with the other; what may be understood at one level as psychological may also be seen as supernatural – 'spiritual' is a word that embraces both. The 'spirits' that Lady Macbeth would pour into her husband's ear (I. 5. 25) are not so different from the 'spirits that tend on mortal thoughts' that she summons to herself. There is a continuous scale from the merely metaphorical – 'Pity, like a naked new-born babe' or 'heaven's cherubin' – through the hallucinatory – the 'air-drawn dagger', which is certainly an illusion, and Banquo's ghost, which probably is (see note to III. 4. 40 s.d.) – to the witches, who clearly have an independent existence. But even this distinction is blurred by the doubts of Macbeth and Banquo about the reality of what they have seen (I. 3. 79–85), and it is a short step from a ghost that is imaginary because its appearance depends on Macbeth's state of mind to real witches who can influence him only because his mind shares the evil that they represent. A debate on the degree to which one may be deceived by imagination was part of the entertainment provided for James at Oxford in 1605, and this may have suggested to Shakespeare the hallucinatory power of Macbeth's imagination, but this fusing of metaphor and reality in the play is characteristic of his dramatic style, and, indeed, of the imagination of the age.

The witches are the 'instruments' of the darkness that Macbeth and his wife invoke, as much the instruments of their dark thoughts as of the dark powers of hell. A Jacobean audience would have been much more ready than we are to believe in their objective existence, but for them, as well as for us, the witches would have personified the unnaturalness of the evil in Macbeth's mind. Its perversion is apparent in their own deformity – they 'should be women' but their beards deny it – and in the mutilated fragments of animals and men from which their charms are brewed, and its sterility in their withered forms and in the blasted heath on which they meet (I. 3. 40–7, 77). Their doctrine reverses the natural order of things: 'Fair is foul, and foul is fair' is the Satanic principle of 'Evil be thou my good'. It echoes in Macbeth's first words (I. 3. 38); he goes on to adopt it in order to gain the throne, and then finds that he cannot escape from it.

The rest of the play explores the implications of this. The confusion of 'fair' with 'foul' is its constant theme; it is emphasised by the heavy irony of Duncan's misjudgement of the two Thanes of Cawdor (I. 4. 11–21) and, in contrast, by his son's elaborate testing of Macduff (see, especially, IV. 3. 23–4). The play is full of false appearances. Macbeth enters a world of false values in which he is guided by deceptive apparitions and hallucinations. His moral sense becomes as confused as are his physical senses when he cannot distinguish the real from the unreal dagger (II. 1. 40–41), and it is the latter that directs him to the murder – he follows unreality. After the murder Lady Macbeth attempts to reassure him with the illusory resemblance between the sleeping and the dead – a recurrent idea in the play (see note to II. 2. 53–4) – but shortly Macduff will summon them from the 'counterfeit' to 'look on death itself' (II. 3. 75–6). There is repeated reference to the murderer's need for deception (I. 5. 62–5, 7. 81–2) and the false appearance that Macbeth thinks to assume temporarily has to become a settled practice; by the time he is planning the murder of Banquo it has become a burden:

> Unsafe the while, that we
> Must . . . make our faces vizards to our hearts,
> Disguising what they are. (III. 2. 32–5)

He has condemned himself to living a lie. The same moral is suggested by the numerous images of clothing in the play, which are generally connected with the adoption of a new or false role (see I. 3. 108–9, 144–6, 7. 34–6, II. 4. 38). By the final scenes the royal robes have become another burden to Macbeth. His title hangs about him 'like a giant's robe/Upon a dwarfish thief', and

He cannot buckle his distempered cause
Within the belt of rule. (V. 2. 21–2, 15–16)

The witches' doctrine is in fact a self-deceiving one. 'Foul is not 'fair', it only appears so; but the first half of their jingle is true, for what should have been 'fair' – kingship – becomes 'foul', polluted by the means by which it was obtained. The witches equivocate with Macbeth in their initial promise to him of 'things that do *sound* so fair' (I. 3. 52), as well as in the prophecies of the apparitions. He achieves the title of king, but finds that he has sold his soul – his 'eternal jewel' (III. 1. 67) – for something that proves worthless. They keep the word of promise to his ear, but break it to his hope.

VII: *THE SYMBOLIC PATTERN*

Macbeth's tragic error is to think that he can assume the unnatural character of evil in order to gain an immediate end, and then put it behind him. He hoped that he could 'trammel up the consequence', but it is the moral consequence which he pretends to ignore, rather than physical revenge, that destroys him. The way in which his crime spreads through and corrupts his reign is reflected in the spreading pattern of imagery in the play, and in the way his earlier words echo through the later scenes and gradually reveal their true meaning. One such ironic sequence comments directly on the impossibility of escaping from one's past deeds. Macbeth had hoped that the murder would be 'done' – over and done with – 'when 'tis done' (I. 7. 1), but when the first murder fails to bring content this phrase is subtly changed, first to the grim resignation of Lady Macbeth's 'what's done is done' (III. 2. 12) and then to her despairing 'What's done cannot be undone' (V. 1. 68).

One suspects that Macbeth really knew this all the time. His outburst when Duncan's murder is discovered (II. 3. 89–94) sounds only half feigned, although it is not until the last act that he realises its full truth, when he sees life as 'a tale/Told by an idiot . . . Signifying nothing' (V. 5. 26–8), and himself as 'fall'n into the sere, the yellow leaf' and deprived of

> that which should accompany old age,
> As honour, love, obedience, troops of friends. (V. 3. 23–6)

Yet the isolation from humanity that he laments here had originally been his own choice. His guilty thoughts had separated him from his companions when he first met the witches, and he had deliberately left the banquet at which he should have been entertaining Duncan in order to brood on his murder; later, when his crimes prevent him from banqueting with his own thanes, he discovers that he has condemned himself to perpetual isolation.

He constantly finds that he is committed to the role of murderer. The images thrown up by his guilty conscience cling to him, like the blood that he fears will never wash off – the 'secret murders sticking on his hands' (V. 2. 17). As his crime was 'unnatural', a perversion of his own being as well as a violation of the natural obligations of a kinsman, a subject and a host (I. 7. 12–16), he carries the consequences in his own nature, and the imagery that expresses this is concerned with the basic requirements of natural life – food, sleep and health. The banquet is a powerful symbol in the play (see introductory notes to I. 7. and III. 4.) and the imagery of food is often associated with that of sleep – 'the season of all natures' (III. 4. 140),

> great nature's second course,
> Chief nourisher in life's feast. (II. 2. 39–40)

The two are explicitly linked by Macbeth and by the Lord to whom Lennox speaks (III. 2. 17–19, 6. 34–5). Deprivation of sleep is the chief symptom of the spiritual and psychological disease that afflicts the Macbeths (see note to II. 2. 36). They have 'infected minds', and their cause is 'distempered' (V. 1. 73, 2. 15). We have already seen how the disorder in their minds is reflected in the state of their kingdom and how this imagery of disease is contrasted with the health-giving powers of the true king (see pp 3–4, and also notes to IV. 2. 17, 3. 165, 170). In her first speech Lady Macbeth had readily described their sin as an 'illness', and the metaphor takes on a terrible reality for them at the end of the play.

With disease goes sterility, which again they had deliberately courted when Macbeth identified himself with 'withered Murder' (II. 1. 52), and Lady Macbeth called on the spirits to unsex her (I. 5. 39–42) and declared her readiness to dash her infant's brains out (I. 7. 54–9); she would change her milk to gall, just as she would eradicate 'th' milk of human kindness' from her husband (I. 5. 47, 16). In consequence, all they achieve is a 'fruitless crown' and a 'barren sceptre' (III. 1. 60–1), symbolising the barrenness of their triumph. As the play proceeds Macbeth's revolt against nature becomes more and more desperate. Unable to destroy 'the seed of Banquo' (III. 1. 69), he would strike against the seeds of life itself. He will 'let the frame of things disjoint' (III. 2. 16); the witches shall answer him

> though the treasure
> Of nature's germens tumble all together,
> Even till destruction sicken. (IV. 1. 58–60)

His initial denial of his own nature has enmeshed him in a course of self-contradiction that leads only to a nihilistic desire for universal chaos.

To balance the forces of disorder and perversion represented by the witches, the play is full of images of natural growth. These are often associated with Banquo, 'the root and father/Of many kings' (III. 1. 5–6); it is he who remarks on the 'procreant cradle' of the temple-haunting martlet, and who first introduces the theme in his demand to the witches –

If you can look into the seeds of time,
And say which grain will grow, and which will not,
Speak then to me. (I. 3. 58–60)

This image is picked up in the next scene by Duncan,

I have begun to plant thee, and will labour
To make thee full of growing,

continued by Banquo,

There if I grow,
The harvest is your own. (I. 4. 28–9, 32–3)

and echoed by Malcolm at the end of play (V. 9. 31). In the later scenes there is a profusion of images of new life, contrasting with 'the sere, the yellow leaf' of Macbeth. The human is linked with natural animal life in an often startling way: Macduff's son is called 'You egg,/Young fry of treachery' (IV. 2. 85–6), Malcolm – the 'sovereign flower' (V. 2. 30) – describes himself as an 'innocent lamb', and Macduff mourns for his 'pretty chickens and their dam' (IV. 3. 16, 218). The youth of Malcolm's army is emphasised (V. 2. 9–11), and exemplified by Young Siward, and when the boughs of Birnam wood are used to conceal their numbers it seems that nature itself is marching against the unnatural tyrant. This symbolism is dominated by the two apparitions of children, the second with a tree in its hand, which foretell and contribute to Macbeth's death, and the thread of metaphor reaches back to his own horrified vision of 'Pity, like a naked new-born babe' as the agent of his destruction. The self-destroying forces of chaos are overthrown by the self-renewing powers of nature, which comprehend both organic physical life and the moral order that is necessary for the health of the social organism.

This intricate interweaving of irony, image and symbol gives the play its imaginative and moral unity. There are many more strands than can be traced in this Introduction, many of which are referred to in the notes – 'blood', for example, is one of the most fertile symbols in the play, there are more than a hundred allusions to it. At the beginning we considered the accidental circumstances that probably influenced Shakespeare in the writing of *Macbeth*, but in the finished play nothing is accidental; every image, sometimes it seems every word, contributes directly to its complex theme. The larger symbolic structure grows organically and inevitably from the character of the hero.

Macbeth was one of the last tragedies that Shakespeare wrote. Of those that preceded it, *Hamlet* presents the most complex and probing study of its hero, while *King Lear* is the most 'universal', stripping human nature to its bare essentials and setting it in the midst of elemental forces. *Macbeth* presents a symbolic pattern, perhaps less inclusive, but as closely knit as that of *Lear*, centred on a character study, less wide in range, but penetrating as deeply as that of *Hamlet*. In *Lear* Shakespeare had shown the innate triumph of goodness, even though its chief representative is hanged at the end of the play. In *Macbeth* he shows the essentially self-defeating character of evil – the unnatural striving to preserve itself by destroying the roots of its own existence.

THE CHARACTERS

DUNCAN, King of Scotland

MALCOLM } his sons
DONALBAIN

MACBETH } commanders of the Scottish army
BANQUO

MACDUFF
LENNOX
ROSS
MENTEITH } Scottish noblemen
ANGUS
CAITHNESS

FLEANCE, Banquo's son.

LADY MACBETH
LADY MACDUFF
BOY, Macduff's son.

SIWARD, Earl of Northumberland, and commander of the English army.
YOUNG SIWARD, his son.

A CAPTAIN
A PORTER
AN OLD MAN
AN ENGLISH DOCTOR
A SCOTTISH DOCTOR
A GENTLEWOMAN, attending on Lady Macbeth
SEYTON, an Officer attending on Macbeth
Three WITCHES
HECATE
The GHOST of BANQUO, and other apparitions

Lords, Gentlemen, Officers, Soldiers, Murderers, Attendants, and Messengers

ACT ONE, scene 1

The witches would enter on a bare stage, perhaps through the trap, with the 'fog and filthy air' suggested by the smoke from burning resin. This brief scene sets the atmosphere of the play, and introduces the forces that control its action. The witches' doctrine of disorder is summed up in the last couplet, and this confusion of moral values is reflected in the tumult in the heavens and the 'hurlyburly' on earth. For the references to witchcraft see pp. 5–7.

2 In thunder . . . rain *As the witches could raise storms they could choose appropriate weather for their meeting.*

3 hurlyburly *tumult – of the insurrection*

4 lost and won *The witches already speak in riddles, and their rhymed octosyllabic verse suggests an incantation.*

8 Graymalkin *The name for a grey cat – 'malkin' was a diminutive of Mary.*

9 Paddock *toad – used here as its name. These are the witches' 'familiars', which would be heard calling off-stage. See p 7.*

10 Anon *At once – I'm coming*

ACT ONE, scene 2

[Alarum within] *Battle call on a trumpet, sounded off-stage. This, with the entry of the Captain, indicates the change from the undefined supernatural setting of scene 1 to the world of military and political action; but the Captain has come from the 'hurlyburly', and his account of the battle emphasises one aspect of the chaos that the witches represent. Consider how Duncan and his court – especially Malcolm (see ll. 3–5) – would receive the Captain.*

1 bloody man *The first of many references to blood in the play. The Captain's speeches plunge us at once into brutal violence, but they are written in a formal 'epic' style, with involved syntax and elaborate similes. Some critics have thought them too artificial in style to have been written by Shakespeare, but, as Coleridge suggested, they are probably intended to contrast with the more realistic verse of the rest of the play – the Captain presents the heroic ideal that Macbeth is going to violate.*

ACT ONE

Scene 1. *Thunder and lightning. Enter three* WITCHES

FIRST WITCH When shall we three meet again?
In thunder, lightning, or in rain?
SECOND WITCH When the hurlyburly's done,
When the battle's lost and won.
THIRD WITCH That will be ere the set of sun.
FIRST WITCH Where the place?
SECOND WITCH Upon the heath.
THIRD WITCH There to meet with Macbeth.
FIRST WITCH I come, Graymalkin.
SECOND WITCH Paddock calls.
THIRD WITCH Anon! 10
ALL Fair is foul, and foul is fair:
Hover through the fog and filthy air.
[*Exeunt*

Scene 2. *Alarum within. Enter* DUNCAN, MALCOLM, DONALBAIN, LENNOX, *with* ATTENDANTS, *meeting a bleeding* CAPTAIN

DUNCAN What bloody man is that? He can report,
As seemeth by his plight, of the revolt
The newest state.
MALCOLM This is the sergeant
Who like a good and hardy soldier fought
'Gainst my captivity. Hail, brave friend!
Say to the King the knowledge of the broil
As thou didst leave it.
CAPTAIN Doubtful it stood,
As two spent swimmers that do cling together
And choke their art. The merciless Macdonwald –
Worthy to be a rebel, for to that 10
The multiplying villainies of nature
Do swarm upon him – from the Western Isles

2 seemeth . . . plight *it seems from his wounded condition*

3 sergeant *'Captain' and 'sergeant' were used indiscriminately to denote subordinate officers.*

5 'Gainst my captivity *To prevent my being taken captive*

6 broil *conflict*

8 spent *exhausted*

9 choke . . . art *impede each other's skill (at swimming)*

10–12 to that . . . him *to that end the vices of human nature breed and swarm upon him – like vermin*

12 Western Isles *Ireland and the Hebrides, off the West coast of Scotland*

13 kerns *light-armed foot-soldiers* gallowglasses *heavy-armed cavalry. Both came from Ireland.*

14–15 Fortune . . . whore *Fortune was often personified as a fickle woman; here she appears to favour the rebel, but, like a prostitute, will be unfaithful to him.*

18 smoked *steamed with blood*

19 minion *favourite, darling*

20 *The short line may be the result of a cut in the text, but the speech may be broken deliberately here to suggest the Captain's exhaustion, as it probably is at l. 41.*

21 Which *Who – probably referring to Macbeth*

shook hands *saluted – he did not waste time in the courtesies of chivalrous combat.*

22 unseamed . . . chops *ripped him open from navel to jaw*

24 cousin *The word was used generally for 'kinsman', but Macbeth was actually Duncan's cousin.*

25–8 'gins his reflection *begins to shine – i.e. in the East, the direction from which the Norwegians attacked. 'Ship-wrecking storms' might recall the witches, and the Captain's words have an obvious ironic application to Macbeth, who is at present the source of comfort for Scotland. 'Mark, King of Scotland' underlines the unintentional warning.*

26 direful *terrifying*

30 skipping *nimble n flight*

31 Norweyan Lord *Sweno, King of Norway*

surveying vantage *observing his opportunity*

32 furbished *polished, fresh*

36 sooth *truth*

37 double cracks *double the normal charges*

39 Except *Unless*

40 memorise . . . Golgotha *make the field of battle as memorable as that of Golgotha – the 'place of the skull', where Christ was crucified.*

Of kerns and gallowglasses is supplied,
And Fortune on his damnéd quarrel smiling
Showed like a rebel's whore. But all's too weak;
For brave Macbeth – well he deserves that name –
Disdaining Fortune, with his brandished steel,
Which smoked with bloody execution,
Like Valour's minion, carved out his passage,
Till he faced the slave; 20
Which ne'er shook hands, nor bade farewell to him,
Till he unseamed him from the nave to th' chops,
And fixed his head upon our battlements.

DUNCAN O valiant cousin, worthy gentleman!

CAPTAIN As whence the sun 'gins his reflection
Shipwrecking storms and direful thunders break,
So from that spring whence comfort seemed to come
Discomfort swells. Mark, King of Scotland, mark:
No sooner Justice had, with Valour armed,
Compelled these skipping kerns to trust their heels, 30
But the Norweyan Lord, surveying vantage,
With furbished arms and new supplies of men,
Began a fresh assault.

DUNCAN Dismayed not this
Our captains, Macbeth and Banquo?

CAPTAIN Yes –
As sparrows eagles, or the hare the lion.
If I say sooth I must report they were
As cannons overcharged with double cracks;
So they doubly redoubled strokes upon the foe.
Except they meant to bathe in reeking wounds,
Or memorise another Golgotha, 40
I cannot tell –
But I am faint, my gashes cry for help.

43–4 *Both his words and his wounds are honourable, and so are equally befitting to him as a soldier.*
smack *taste*

45 Thane *A Scottish title, next in rank beneath that of Earl (see V. 9. 28–30).*

47 seems to *looks as if he were about to*

49 flout *insult. The threat was so great that Ross speaks as if it still hung over them, using the historic present tense.*
50 fan . . . cold *turn them cold with fear*
51 Norway *i.e. the King of Norway*
53 dismal *threatening disaster*
54 Bellona's bridegroom *Macbeth; Bellona was the Roman goddess of war.*
capped in proof *clad in tested – 'proved' – armour*
55 Confronted . . . comparisons *Faced him with a courage and strength equal to his own. As Macbeth's arm is also soon to become rebellious, there is further irony in this precise comparison between him and Scotland's enemy.*
57 Curbing *Checking*
lavish *excessive, overweening*
60 craves composition *begs for terms of peace*
62 Saint Colme's Inch *Inchcolm, an island in the Firth of Forth*
63 dollars *Dutch coins, worth about 15p. They were current in England at the beginning of the seventeenth century.*
64–6 *Duncan's emphasis on 'that' Thane of Cawdor anticipates the dramatic irony of I. 4. 11–21.*
65 bosom interest *affectionate trust ('interest in him') or, perhaps, the interests that are closest to my heart*
present *immediate*
68 lost . . . won *A faint, but ominous, echo of the witches (I. 1. 4). The irony of I. 4. 11–21 is again anticipated: Macbeth will not only gain the title that Cawdor has lost, but succeed where he failed, in secret treachery.*

DUNCAN So well thy words become thee as thy wounds,
They smack of honour both. Go get him surgeons.

[*Exit* CAPTAIN, *attended*

Enter ROSS *and* ANGUS

Who comes here?

MALCOLM The worthy Thane of Ross.

LENNOX What a haste looks through his eyes! So should he look
That seems to speak things strange.

ROSS God save the King!

DUNCAN Whence camest thou, worthy Thane?

ROSS From Fife, great King,
Where the Norweyan banners flout the sky,
And fan our people cold. 50
Norway himself, with terrible numbers,
Assisted by that most disloyal traitor,
The Thane of Cawdor, began a dismal conflict,
Till that Bellona's bridegroom, lapped in proof,
Confronted him with self-comparisons,
Point against point, rebellious arm 'gainst arm,
Curbing his lavish spirit; and, to conclude,
The victory fell on us.

DUNCAN Great happiness!

ROSS That now
Sweno, the Norways' King, craves composition. 60
Nor would we deign him burial of his men
Till he disbursèd, at Saint Colme's Inch,
Ten thousand dollars to our general use.

DUNCAN No more that Thane of Cawdor shall deceive
Our bosom interest. Go pronounce his present death,
And with his former title greet Macbeth.

ROSS I'll see it done.

DUNCAN What he hath lost, noble Macbeth hath won.

[*Exeunt*

ACT ONE, scene 3

2 Killing swine *Probably to avenge some insult*

6 Aroint thee *Be off!*
rump-fed *either fat-rumped, or well fed*
ronyon *scabby wretch*

7 master . . . Tiger *A ship of the same name was in the news in 1606. It reached Milford Haven in June after a voyage that had been dogged by misfortune, including the death of its master.*

8 in a sieve *See p 5.*

9 rat . . . tail *An appropriate form in which to creep on board a ship. When witches were transformed into animals they were generally deficient of a tail as there is no corresponding part of the human anatomy – another example of the distortion of nature that the witches represent.*

10 I'll do *i.e. take revenge – a gesture might indicate how. The phrase is repeated thrice as three was a magic number – and nine even more potent (see ll. 22, 35–6).*

15 they blow *from which they blow, so preventing the ship from entering port*

16 quarters *i.e. of the compass*

17 shipman's card *compass card*

20 penthouse lid *eyelid – it slopes like the roof of a penthouse, or lean-to shed*

21 forbid *under a curse*

22 sev'n-nights *weeks. The voyage of the Tiger lasted just one day more than eighty-one weeks.*

23 peak *waste away*

24 Though . . . lost *The limitation on the witches' power is important in assessing their influence on Macbeth. In some respect his fate resembles that of the master – he is deprived of sleep, drained 'dry as hay', and metaphorically 'tempest-tossed' – but as he fails to resist their temptations he is completely lost.*

Scene 3. *Thunder. Enter the three* WITCHES

FIRST WITCH Where has thou been, sister?
SECOND WITCH Killing swine.
THIRD WITCH Sister, where thou?
FIRST WITCH A sailor's wife had chestnuts in her lap,
And munched, and munched, and munched – 'Give me,' quoth I.
'Aroint thee, witch!' the rump-fed ronyon cries.
Her husband's to Aleppo gone, master o' the *Tiger*;
But in a sieve I'll thither sail,
And like a rat without a tail,
I'll do, I'll do, and I'll do. 10
SECOND WITCH I'll give thee a wind.
FIRST WITCH Th' art kind.
THIRD WITCH And I another.
FIRST WITCH I myself have all the other;
And the very ports they blow,
All the quarters that they know
I' the shipman's card.
I'll drain him dry as hay;
Sleep shall neither night nor day
Hang upon his penthouse lid; 20
He shall live a man forbid.
Weary sev'n-nights nine times nine
Shall he dwindle, peak, and pine.
Though his bark cannot be lost,
Yet it shall be tempest-tossed.
Look what I have.
SECOND WITCH Show me, show me.
FIRST WITCH Here I have a pilot's thumb,
Wrecked as homeward he did come.
[*Drum within*
THIRD WITCH A drum, a drum! 30
Macbeth doth come.

32 Weird Sisters *See p 6.*

33 Posters *Swift travellers – this meaning of 'post' survives in 'post-haste'.*

37 the charm's . . . up *the spell is completed, ready to operate – with an allusion to the circling movements with which they concluded its preparation.*

38 So . . . seen *Macbeth's first words echo the witches' incantation (I. 1. 11). He may refer to the changing fortunes of the battle, or to the sudden change in the weather – the witches having raised their own local thunderstorm.*

39 called *said to be*

42–3 aught . . . question *It was dangerous to question some supernatural beings (see IV. 1. 74–5).*

44–5 her . . . lips *They refuse to answer Banquo.*
choppy *chapped*

48 Glamis *Now pronounced 'Glams', but in the play as two syllables.*

52 sound so fair *Banquo's phrase immediately relates the prophecies to the uncertainty that already surrounds 'foul' and 'fair'.*

53 fantastical *unreal, creations of the fancy*

54 show *appear*

55 present grace *the dignity he already possesses – Thane of Glamis*

56 noble having *possession of nobility – the dignity they have predicted for him, Thane of Cawdor*

57 rapt *entranced, taken out of himself – the state of 'ecstasy' (see III. 2. 22 and note)*

58 seeds of time *the seeds from which future events will grow*

ALL The Weird Sisters, hand in hand,
Posters of the sea and land,
Thus do go about, about,
Thrice to thine, and thrice to mine,
And thrice again, to make up nine.
Peace! – the charm's wound up.

Enter MACBETH *and* BANQUO

MACBETH So foul and fair a day I have not seen.
BANQUO How far is't called to Forres? What are these,
So withered, and so wild in their attire, 40
That look not like th' inhabitants o' th' earth,
And yet are on't? Live you? Or are you aught
That man may question? You seem to understand me,
By each at once her choppy finger laying
Upon her skinny lips. You should be women,
And yet your beards forbid me to interpret
That you are so.
MACBETH Speak, if you can; what are you?
FIRST WITCH All hail, Macbeth! Hail to thee, Thane of Glamis!
SECOND WITCH All hail, Macbeth! Hail to thee, Thane of Cawdor!
THIRD WITCH All hail, Macbeth, that shalt be King hereafter! 50
BANQUO Good sir, why do you start, and seem to fear
Things that do sound so fair? I' th' name of truth,
Are ye fantastical, or that indeed
Which outwardly ye show? My noble partner
You greet with present grace, and great prediction
Of noble having and of royal hope,
That he seems rapt withal. To me you speak not.
If you can look into the seeds of time,
And say which grain will grow, and which will not,

67 get *beget*

70 imperfect *leaving much unsaid. The witches are about to disappear.*

71 Sinel *Macbeth's father.*

73 A prosperous gentleman *Macbeth has evidently not heard of Cawdor's treachery; we learn later that he helped the rebels secretly (ll. 111–14).*

74 Stands . . . belief *Does not fall within the scope of what may be believed*

76 owe *own, come into possession of*

strange *The word is often used in the play with the sense of 'unnatural'.*

intelligence *information*

77 blasted *i.e. by lightning and storms – perhaps raised by supernatural forces*

78 [WITCHES vanish] *This would probably have been effected by the use of the trap and stage fog.*

81 corporal *corporeal*

84 insane root *root that can cause insanity – probably henbane or hemlock*

88 To . . . words *Banquo replies lightheartedly, interpreting Macbeth's 'went it not so?' as if he were trying to remember a song. See p 9.*

Speak then to me, who neither beg nor fear 60
Your favours nor your hate.

FIRST WITCH Hail!

SECOND WITCH Hail!

THIRD WITCH Hail!

FIRST WITCH Lesser than Macbeth, and greater.

SECOND WITCH Not so happy, yet much happier.

THIRD WITCH Thou shalt get kings, though thou be none.
So all hail, Macbeth and Banquo!

FIRST WITCH Banquo and Macbeth, all hail!

MACBETH Stay, you imperfect speakers, tell me more. 70
By Sinel's death I know I am Thane of Glamis,
But how of Cawdor? The Thane of Cawdor lives,
A prosperous gentleman; and to be king
Stands not within the prospect of belief,
No more than to be Cawdor. Say from whence
You owe this strange intelligence, or why
Upon this blasted heath you stop our way
With such prophetic greeting. Speak, I charge you. [WITCHES *vanish*

BANQUO The earth hath bubbles, as the water has,
And these are of them. Whither are they vanished? 80

MACBETH Into the air; and what seemed corporal melted
As breath into the wind. Would they had stayed!

BANQUO Were such things here as we do speak about,
Or have we eaten on the insane root
That takes the reason prisoner?

MACBETH Your children shall be kings.

BANQUO You shall be king.

MACBETH And Thane of Cawdor too; went it not so?

BANQUO To the selfsame tune and words. Who's here?

Enter ROSS *and* ANGUS

ROSS The King hath happily received, Macbeth,
The news of thy success; and when he reads 90

91 venture *perilous enterprise, i.e. Macbeth's personal combat with Macdonwald*

92–3 His wonders . . . his *An obscure statement: the general sense is that his wonder is so great that it conflicts with his desire to praise Macbeth – he does not know whether to express his own amazement or the praise due to Macbeth, knowing that it will be inadequate.*

97 Strange . . . death *The corpses of the rebels – their unnatural ('strange') postures and expressions are images of death. There is a contrast between Macbeth's courage here and his later fear of the 'stranger' images of death that he creates – the corpse of Duncan and the ghost of Banquo. Compare III. 4. 60.*

hail *The Folio has 'tale', perhaps in the sense of 'tally'; 'as thick as tale' might thus mean 'as fast as they could be counted', but the emendation seems more probable. The metaphor is continued by 'poured' (l. 100).*

98 post *messenger*

104 earnest *pledge*

of a greater honour *We do not know what Duncan has in mind, but Macbeth must have thought of the throne.*

106 addition *title added to one's name*

107 What . . . true? *In what tone would Banquo say this?*

108–9 Why . . . robes? *The first of many images in the play connected with clothes.*

110 heavy judgement *sentence of death*

112 line *strengthen – continuing the metaphor of clothing*

113 vantage *support*

114 wrack *destruction*

115 capital *punishable by death*

117 is behind *is to come*

pains *trouble*

Thy personal venture in the rebels' fight,
His wonders and his praises do contend
Which should be thine or his. Silenced with that,
In viewing o'er the rest o' th' selfsame day,
He finds thee in the stout Norweyan ranks,
Nothing afeard of what thyself didst make,
Strange images of death. As thick as hail
Came post with post, and every one did bear
Thy praises in his kingdom's great defence,
And poured them down before him.

ANGUS We are sent 100
To give thee from our royal master thanks;
Only to herald thee into his sight,
Not pay thee.

ROSS And, for an earnest of a greater honour,
He bade me, from him, call thee Thane of Cawdor;
In which addition, hail, most worthy Thane,
For it is thine.

BANQUO [*Aside*] What, can the devil speak true?

MACBETH The Thane of Cawdor lives. Why do you dress me
In borrowed robes?

ANGUS Who was the Thane lives yet,
But under heavy judgement bears that life 110
Which he deserves to lose. Whether he was combined
With those of Norway, or did line the rebel
With hidden help and vantage, or that with both
He laboured in his country's wrack, I know not;
But treasons capital, confessed and proved,
Have overthrown him.

MACBETH [*Aside*] Glamis, and Thane of Cawdor;
The greatest is behind. [*To* ROSS *and* ANGUS] Thanks for your pains.
[*Aside to* BANQUO] Do you not hope your children shall be kings,

120 trusted home *believed in completely*

121 enkindle *fire, excite your hopes. Does Banquo still speak lightheartedly or does he suspect that he is voicing Macbeth's thoughts?*

123 win . . . harm *entice us to our destruction*

124 instruments of darkness *agents of evil*

125 honest trifles *unimportant truths*

126 deepest consequence *matters of greatest importance. Does Banquo speak the last four lines to himself or to Macbeth; what difference would it make to the way in which he says them?*

127 Cousins *Comrades*

128–9 swelling . . . theme *majestic drama on the theme of kingship. The use of images from the stage – 'prologues', 'act', 'theme' – may hint that Macbeth will achieve only the illusion of kingship; compare his expression of disillusionment (V. 5. 24–6). The word 'swelling' suggests the unfolding of the drama, the majesty of kingship and the inflation of Macbeth's ambition.*

130 soliciting *prompting, persuasion*

131 Cannot . . . good *His thoughts readily chime in with the riddling contradictions that are at the centre of the witches' evil creed.*

132 earnest *pledges*

135 unfix my hair *make it stand on end*

136 seated *firmly fixed*

137 Against . . . nature *In an unnatural way*

Present fears *Causes of fear which already exist*

139 whose . . . fantastical *in which murder is only imaginary*

140 Shakes . . . man *Disrupts the unity of my personality. 'State of man' suggests the correspondence between the constitution of a man and that of a kingdom (see p 3). 'Single' might also mean 'weak' (see I. 6. 16).*

140–1 function . . . surmise *powers of action are overwhelmed by speculation about the future*

141–2 nothing . . . not *he is so preoccupied with future events, although they have no actual existence, that nothing else exists for him*

142 rapt *entranced – see note to l. 57. Consider what Banquo, Ross and Angus have been talking about; it would affect their behaviour while Macbeth soliloquises.*

145 strange *unfamiliar, new*

cleave . . . mould *do not fit the body. Is Banquo's remark guileless, or is he inventing an excuse for Macbeth?*

When those that gave the Thane of Cawdor to
me
Promised no less to them?

BANQUO [*Aside to* MACBETH] That, trusted home, 120
Might yet enkindle you unto the crown,
Besides the Thane of Cawdor. But 'tis strange;
And oftentimes, to win us to our harm,
The instruments of darkness tell us truths,
Win us with honest trifles, to betray 's
In deepest consequence.
[*To* ROSS *and* ANGUS] Cousins, a word I pray you.

MACBETH [*Aside*] Two truths are told
As happy prologues to the swelling act
Of the imperial theme. [*Aloud*] I thank you,
gentlemen.
[*Aside*] This supernatural soliciting 130
Cannot be ill, cannot be good. If ill,
Why hath it given me earnest of success,
Commencing in a truth? I am Thane of
Cawdor.
If good, why do I yield to that suggestion
Whose horrid image doth unfix my hair,
And make my seated heart knock at my ribs,
Against the use of nature? Present fears
Are less than horrible imaginings:
My thought, whose murder yet is but fantastical,
Shakes so my single state of man that function 140
Is smothered in surmise, and nothing is
But what is not.

BANQUO Look how our partner's rapt.

MACBETH [*Aside*] If chance will have me king, why,
chance may crown me,
Without my stir.

BANQUO New honours come upon him,
Like our strange garments, cleave not to their
mould
But with the aid of use.

147 Time . . . day *The stormiest day will come to an end. Does this suggest that Macbeth has reached a decision?*
148 stay . . . leisure *await your readiness*
149 Give . . . favour *Pardon me*
wrought *worked upon, agitated*

151 registered *recorded in the book of memory*

153 at . . . time *when we have more time*
154 interim . . . it *having considered it in the meantime*
155 free *sincere*

ACT ONE, scene 4

[Flourish] *A fanfare. The courtly tone of this scene is evident in the formality of the speeches, especially Duncan's – here, very much 'the gracious Duncan' (III. 1. 65) – and would be reflected in the formal groupings on the stage. The ceremony expresses the natural order in the kingdom, the loyal and affectionate dependence of the nobles on the King, which is twice compared with the relationship of children to a father (ll. 25, 35). Its naturalness is also emphasised by the images of growth (ll. 28–33), suggesting the prosperity that results.*

2 in commission *charged with the execution*
6 set forth *exhibited*
8 Became him *So befitted him. This account of Cawdor's death may have been suggested by the dignified bearing of Sir Everard Digby at his execution for complicity in the Gunpowder Plot.*
9 studied *rehearsed*
10 owed *owned*
11 careless *not worthy of care. These lines might be recalled at the end of the play when the next Thane of Cawdor, Macbeth, also regards life as a 'careless trifle' (see V. 5. 19–28).*
11–12 art . . . face *technique by which to discover a man's cast of thought by the expression on his face*

MACBETH [*Aside*] Come what come may,
Time and the hour runs through the roughest day.
BANQUO Worthy Macbeth, we stay upon your leisure.
MACBETH Give me your favour; my dull brain was wrought
With things forgotten. Kind gentlemen, your pains 150
Are registered where every day I turn
The leaf to read them. Let us toward the King.
[*Aside to* BANQUO] Think upon what hath chanced; and at more time,
The interim having weighed it, let us speak
Our free hearts each to other.
BANQUO Very gladly.
MACBETH Till then, enough. – Come, friends. [*Exeunt*

Scene 4. *Flourish. Enter* DUNCAN, MALCOLM, DONALBAIN, LENNOX, *and* ATTENDANTS

DUNCAN Is execution done on Cawdor? Are not
Those in commission yet returned?
MALCOLM My liege,
They are not yet come back; but I have spoke
With one that saw him die, who did report
That very frankly he confessed his treasons,
Implored your Highness' pardon, and set forth
A deep repentance. Nothing in his life
Became him like the leaving it; he died
As one that had been studied in his death,
To throw away the dearest thing he owed 10
As 'twere a careless trifle.
DUNCAN There's no art
To find the mind's construction in the face:
He was a gentleman on whom I built

14 [Enter MACBETH] *His first appearance in the formal atmosphere of the court, battle stained and fresh from his encounter with the witches, is full of dramatic irony (see p 13). This is the one point in the play at which Duncan might be thought to show the negligence with which Holinshed charged him (see p 8), although his trust is seen as a virtue rather than a vice.*

16 Thou . . . before *Your deserts are so far in advance of your reward*

17 swiftest . . . recompense *the most prompt reward*

19–20 the proportion . . . mine *I could have thanked and rewarded you in proportion to your deserts.*

21 more than all *i.e. more than all I possess*

23 pays itself *is its own reward*

25 children and servants *as children and servants, i.e. affectionate and loyal*

27 Safe toward *With a sure regard for – or, to ensure the safety of you, whom we love*

34 Wanton *Unrestrained*

36 nearest *i.e. to the throne. Macbeth was in fact the nearest after Duncan's own sons.*

37 establish . . . estate *settle the succession*

39 Prince of Cumberland *The title bestowed on the heir to the throne. Scotland held Cumberland as a fief from England.*

41 signs of nobleness *titles and honours*

50

An absolute trust.

Enter MACBETH, BANQUO, ROSS, *and* ANGUS

O worthiest cousin!
The sin of my ingratitude even now
Was heavy on me. Thou art so far before
That swiftest wing of recompense is slow
To overtake thee. Would thou hadst less deserved,
That the proportion both of thanks and payment
Might have been mine. Only I have left to say, 20
More is thy due than more than all can pay.

MACBETH The service and the loyalty I owe,
In doing it, pays itself. Your Highness' part
Is to receive our duties; and our duties
Are to your throne and state, children and servants,
Which do but what they should by doing every thing
Safe toward your love and honour.

DUNCAN Welcome hither.
I have begun to plant thee, and will labour
To make thee full of growing. – Noble Banquo,
That hast no less deserved, nor must be known 30
No less to have done so, let me infold thee,
And hold thee to my heart.

BANQUO There if I grow,
The harvest is your own.

DUNCAN My plenteous joys,
Wanton in fulness, seek to hide themselves
In drops of sorrow. – Sons, kinsmen, thanes,
And you whose places are the nearest, know,
We will establish our estate upon
Our eldest, Malcolm, whom we name hereafter
The Prince of Cumberland; which honour must
Not unaccompanied invest him only, 40
But signs of nobleness, like stars, shall shine

42 Inverness *i.e. Macbeth's castle*
43 bind us *increase our debt*
44 The rest . . . you *Leisure is irksome when it is not used in your service.*
45 harbinger *Court officer who preceded the king to arrange for his lodging*

52 wink at *be closed to, not see*
let that be *let the action be performed*

55 in . . . fed *praise of Macbeth is like a feast to Duncan.*

57 care *consideration for my welfare*

ACT ONE, scene 5

The scene would probably change from the platform to the inner stage.

2 perfectest report *most reliable information*

5 rapt *entranced.*
6 missives *messengers*

9 coming . . . time *future*
10 deliver thee *report to you*

On all deservers. [*To* MACBETH] From hence to Inverness,
And bind us further to you.

MACBETH The rest is labour, which is not used for you.
I'll be myself the harbinger, and make joyful
The hearing of my wife with your approach;
So humbly take my leave.

DUNCAN My worthy Cawdor!

MACBETH [*Aside*] The Prince of Cumberland! That is a step
On which I must fall down, or else o'erleap,
For in my way it lies. Stars, hide your fires,
Let not light see my black and deep desires;
The eye wink at the hand; yet let that be
Which the eye fears, when it is done, to see.
[*Exit*

DUNCAN True, worthy Banquo; he is full so valiant,
And in his commendations I am fed:
It is a banquet to me. Let's after him,
Whose care is gone before to bid us welcome.
It is a peerless kinsman. [*Flourish. Exeunt*

Scene 5. *Enter* LADY MACBETH, *reading a letter*

LADY MACBETH *They met me in the day of success; and I have learned by the perfectest report they have more in them than mortal knowledge. When I burned in desire to question them further, they made themselves air, into which they vanished. Whiles I stood rapt in the wonder of it, came missives from the King, who all-hailed me "Thane of Cawdor", by which title before these Weird Sisters saluted me, and referred me to the coming on of time with "Hail, King that shalt be!" This have I thought good to deliver thee, my dearest* 10 *partner of greatness, that thou mightst not lose the*

12 dues of rejoicing *your share of rejoicing*

13 Lay . . . heart *Treasure it up – or, ponder on it. Which is preferred depends on how far one thinks Macbeth was contemplating murder when he wrote the letter. It is noteworthy that he does not mention the promises made to Banquo.*

16 milk . . . kindness *softness of human nature – 'kindness' has the same meaning as 'kind' in 'humankind', although it also carries the meaning of 'kindly'. For Lady Macbeth 'milk' stands for effeminacy (see l. 47); she ignores its life-giving power.*

17 catch *seize on*

nearest *most expeditious*

19 illness . . . it *evil that must accompany it. It is characteristic that from the start Lady Macbeth acknowledges evil to be disease (see p 28); for her 'foul is fair'.*

19–20 What . . . holily *She also slips, like Macbeth (I. 3. 131), only more readily, into the condensed, antithetical style of the witches. 'Highly' can refer both to the 'high' dignities he desires and to the intensity of the desire.*

21–4 Thou'dst . . . undone *'That' in l. 22 is the crown, and in l. 23 the murder; both are the objects of 'have' in l. 21. She knows her husband well (compare I. 4. 52–3).*

26 chastise *drive out*

27 golden round *crown*

28 metaphysical *supernatural*

29 withal *with*

30 Thou'rt . . . it *Why does she respond in this way?*

32 informed . . . preparation *informed me so that I could make preparations*

34 had the speed of *rode with more speed*

37 raven *a bird of ill-omen*

dues of rejoicing by being ignorant of what greatness is promised thee. Lay it to thy heart, and farewell.

Glamis thou art, and Cawdor; and shalt be
What thou art promised. Yet do I fear thy nature;
It is too full o' th' milk of human kindness
To catch the nearest way. Thou wouldst be great,
Art not without ambition, but without
The illness should attend it. What thou wouldst highly,
That wouldst thou holily; wouldst not play false, 20
And yet wouldst wrongly win. Thou'dst have, great Glamis,
That which cries 'Thus thou must do' if thou have it;
And that which rather thou dost fear to do
Than wishest should be undone. Hie thee hither,
That I may pour my spirits in thine ear,
And chastise with the valour of my tongue
All that impedes thee from the golden round,
Which fate and metaphysical aid doth seem
To have thee crowned withal.

Enter a MESSENGER

What is your tidings?

MESSENGER The King comes here tonight.

LADY MACBETH Thou'rt mad to say it. 30
Is not thy master with him – who, were't so,
Would have informed for preparation?

MESSENGER So please you, it is true; our Thane is coming.
One of my fellows had the speed of him,
Who, almost dead for breath, had scarcely more
Than would make up his message.

LADY MACBETH Give him tending;
He brings great news. [*Exit* MESSENGER
The raven himself is hoarse
That croaks the fatal entrance of Duncan

39–40 spirits . . . thoughts *spirits, like the witches' familiars, who watch for and encourage thoughts of murder*

40 unsex me *destroy my femininity*

42 Make . . . blood *Make me insensitive – by clogging up the means of communication between her heart, the seat of feeling, and her other faculties.*

43 access *means of entrance*

remorse *pity. Pity must be prevented from intruding into her thoughts.*

44 compunctious . . . nature *natural scruples of conscience*

45 fell *fierce*

45–6 keep . . . it *come between my purpose and my putting it into effect – as someone might interpose himself between two combatants in order to 'keep the peace'*

47 for gall *turn it into gall – or, feed upon it as if it were gall*

murd'ring ministers *the spirits of l. 39. Familiars were supposed to suck the witches' breasts.*

48 sightless *invisible*

49 wait . . . mischief *assist the malign forces in nature*

thick *opaque. Her invocation echoes that of Macbeth (I. 4. 50–3).*

50 pall *shroud*

dunnest *darkest*

51 my . . . knife *This suggests that she intends to kill Duncan herself, but she may only be speaking figuratively, and her later statements to the same effect (ll. 66–7, 72) may only be to reassure Macbeth.*

53–4 Great . . . hereafter *She again echoes the witches in their greeting of Macbeth.*

56–7 I feel . . . instant *Like Macbeth (I. 3. 137–42) she experiences the future as if it already existed in the (present) instant.*

57–9 *This tense interchange is full of sinister implications, but Macbeth's words are open to various interpretation. Is 'as he purposes' said innocently or ominously?*

62–3 To beguile . . . time *To deceive the company present at any particular time adapt your looks to the present circumstances.*

64–5 look . . . under't *A medallion with this design was struck to commemorate the discovery of the Gunpowder Plot. It also recalls the serpent that persuaded Eve to tempt Adam, as Lady Macbeth tempts her husband.*

67 dispatch *management – with a grim pun on the 'dispatching' of Duncan, which continues the innuendo of 'provided for' in the previous line.*

Under my battlements. Come, you spirits
That tend on mortal thoughts, unsex me here, 40
And fill me, from the crown to the toe, top-full
Of direst cruelty. Make thick my blood,
Stop up th' access and passage to remorse,
That no compunctious visitings of nature
Shake my fell purpose, nor keep peace between
The effect and it. Come to my woman's breasts,
And take my milk for gall, you murd'ring ministers,
Wherever in your sightless substances
You wait on nature's mischief. Come, thick night,
And pall thee in the dunnest smoke of hell, 50
That my keen knife see not the wound it makes,
Nor heaven peep through the blanket of the dark,
To cry 'Hold, hold!'

Enter MACBETH

Great Glamis! worthy Cawdor!
Greater than both, by the all-hail hereafter!
Thy letters have transported me beyond
This ignorant present, and I feel now
The future in the instant.

MACBETH My dearest love,
Duncan comes here tonight.

LADY MACBETH And when goes hence?

MACBETH Tomorrow, as he purposes.

LADY MACBETH O, never
Shall sun that morrow see! 60
Your face, my Thane, is as a book where men
May read strange matters. To beguile the time,
Look like the time; bear welcome in your eye,
Your hand, your tongue; look like the innocent flower,
But be the serpent under't. He that's coming
Must be provided for; and you shall put
This night's great business into my dispatch,

69 solely *nothing but*

70 We . . . further *What does this suggest about Macbeth's attitude to the murder?*

clear *with an open countenance*

71 To alter . . . fear *To change countenance is always a sign of fear*

ACT ONE, scene 6

[Hautboys] *an early form of oboe.*

[torches] *torch bearers, who would be needed to give light within the castle. They add to the contrast between the darkness within and the light without (see pp 17–18). The castle itself is looking 'like the innocent flower', with only the martlets in evidence, the ravens croaking behind the battlements!*

1 seat *situation*

2 Nimbly *Freshly*

2–3 recommends . . . senses *ingratiates itself by soothing my refined senses – 'gentle' refers both to the air and to his senses. 'Recommends' has sinister overtones of flattery.*

4 temple-haunting *frequenting churches*

martlet *house-martin. Caroline Spurgeon points out that 'martin' was a slang term for 'dupe', and that Shakespeare's other reference to martins* (Merchant of Venice, *II. 9. 28*) *is also associated with a guest who is to be deceived.*

approve *gives proof*

5 loved mansionry *the nests that it delights to build here*

6 wooingly *invitingly*

jutty *projection*

7 coign of vantage *convenient corner*

8 pendent *hanging*

procreant *in which it breeds*

11–12 The love . . . love *The love with which I am attended can be a nuisance, but I am still grateful for it because it is love. (He uses the royal plural.)*

13 'ield *yield, in its older sense of 'reward'. By his example he instructs her to ask God to reward him for the trouble ('pains') he is causing her, because it too is prompted by love.*

15 In . . . done *Performed twice over, in every respect*

16 single *weak, simple*

contend *compete*

18 those of old *former honours*

Which shall to all our nights and days to come
Give solely sovereign sway and masterdom.

MACBETH We will speak further.

LADY MACBETH Only look up clear; 70
To alter favour ever is to fear.
Leave all the rest to me. [*Exeunt*

Scene 6. *Hautboys and torches. Enter* DUNCAN, MALCOLM, DONALBAIN, BANQUO, LENNOX, MACDUFF, ROSS, ANGUS, *and* ATTENDANTS

DUNCAN This castle hath a pleasant seat; the air
Nimbly and sweetly recommends itself
Unto our gentle senses.

BANQUO This guest of summer,
The temple-haunting martlet, does approve
By his loved mansionry that the heaven's breath
Smells wooingly here: no jutty, frieze,
Buttress, nor coign of vantage, but this bird
Hath made his pendent bed and procreant cradle.
Where they most breed and haunt, I have observed
The air is delicate.

Enter LADY MACBETH

DUNCAN See, see, our honoured hostess. 10
The love that follows us sometime is our trouble,
Which still we thank as love. Herein I teach you,
How you shall bid God 'ield us for your pains,
And thank us for your trouble.

LADY MACBETH All our service,
In every point twice done, and then done double,
Were poor and single business to contend
Against those honours deep and broad wherewith
Your Majesty loads our house. For those of old,

19 late *recent*
20 rest . . . hermits *always remain offering grateful prayers for you – like beadsmen, who were paid to offer prayers for the dead. (There is a veiled threat in her words.)*
21 coursed . . . heels *followed him closely – as a hare is coursed*
22 purveyor *An officer who preceded the king to arrange for provisions – compare 'harbinger' (I. 4. 45).*
23 holp *helped*
26 theirs *their servants*
in compt *on account – she continues the theme of I. 4. – that all their titles and possessions are held in trust from the king.*
27 make . . . audit *account accurately for their possessions*
28 Still *Always*
31 By . . . leave *Allow me. He may usher her into the castle, or, as Granville Barker suggests, kiss her.*

ACT ONE, scene 7

[SEWER] *chief server, major-domo.*
[divers] *various.*
The procession of servants suggests the ceremonial order of the feast, which should be remembered throughout the scene as a symbol of the social order and human fellowship from which Macbeth excludes himself. Duncan's metaphorical use of 'banquet' (I. 4. 54–6) has already suggested its wider symbolic significance.

1 were done *over and done with*
2 It . . . quickly *Perhaps an echo of Christ's words to Judas, 'That thou doest, do quickly'* (John, *xiii.* 27). *This is Duncan's 'last supper'.*
2–3 If . . . consequence *If the murder could itself prevent any further consequences.*
3 trammel up *entangle, as in a net*
catch *achieve, secure – continuing the image suggested by 'trammel up'*
4 surcease *cessation – either the termination of Duncan's life or the conclusion of the act of murder ('his' was often used for 'its').*
that . . . blow *so that this blow alone*
6 bank . . . time *temporal life, seen as a sand-bank in the sea of eternity. The Folio has 'bank and school'.*

And the late dignities heaped up to them,
We rest your hermits.

DUNCAN Where's the Thane of Cawdor? 20
We coursed him at the heels, and had a purpose
To be his purveyor; but he rides well,
And his great love, sharp as his spur, hath holp him
To his home before us. Fair and noble hostess,
We are your guest tonight.

LADY MACBETH Your servants ever
Have theirs, themselves, and what is theirs, in compt,
To make their audit at your Highness' pleasure,
Still to return your own.

DUNCAN Give me your hand;
Conduct me to mine host. We love him highly,
And shall continue our graces towards him. 30
By your leave, hostess. [*Exeunt*

Scene 7. *Hautboys and torches. Enter, and pass over the stage, a* SEWER, *and divers* SERVANTS *with dishes and service. Then enter* MACBETH

MACBETH If it were done, when 'tis done, then 'twere well
It were done quickly. If the assassination
Could trammel up the consequence, and catch,
With his surcease, success; that but this blow
Might be the be-all and the end-all – here,
But here, upon this bank and shoal of time –
We'd jump the life to come. But in these cases
We still have judgement here – that we but teach
Bloody instructions, which, being taught, return
To plague th' inventor. This even-handed justice 10

7 jump *skip over, ignore*
life to come *eternal life, with the possibility of punishment after death*
8–9 that . . . instructions *in that we only teach others how to murder*
10 even-handed *fairly balanced*
11 Commends *Recommends, prescribes*
ingredience *mixture*
chalice *ornamental cup, used in religious rites*
14 Strong both *Both are strong reasons*
17 borne *exercised*
faculties *the powers of the crown*
18 clear *guiltless*
19–20 Will . . . taking-off *The image recalls the morality plays (see p 12). 'Plead' continues the language of a law court (see 'cases', 'judgement' and 'instructions'), but now with the suggestion of the Day of Judgement – Macbeth's imagination cannot 'jump the life to come'.*
20 taking-off *murder*
22 Striding *Bestriding.*
blast *The storm of horror – suggested by 'trumpet-tongued'.*
cherubin *The highest order of angels, often represented as winged children. Compare* Psalms, *xviii. 10.*
23 sightless couriers *invisible messengers, i.e. the winds*
24 blow . . . eye *i.e. like dust, causing tears*
25 tears . . . wind *The wind often drops when rain falls.*
25–8 I have . . . other *Continuing the metaphor of riding, ambition is first the spur to stimulate his purpose, and then either the horse that is urged to leap too high, or the rider who leaps too vigorously into the saddle and falls on the other side. Compare I. 4. 49.*
32–3 bought . . . opinions *gained the highest esteem*

34 would be worn *ought to be worn – the imagery of clothes is continued by Lady Macbeth in l. 36*
35 Was . . . drunk *Was the hope only stimulated by drink?*

37 green and pale *suffering a hangover*
38 freely *readily*
39 Such . . . love *i.e. as fickle*

Commends th' ingredience of our poisoned chalice
To our own lips. He's here in double trust:
First, as I am his kinsman and his subject –
Strong both against the deed; then, as his host,
Who should against his murderer shut the door,
Not bear the knife myself. Besides, this Duncan
Hath borne his faculties so meek, hath been
So clear in his great office, that his virtues
Will plead like angels trumpet-tongued against
The deep damnation of his taking-off; 20
And Pity, like a naked new-born babe,
Striding the blast, or heaven's cherubin, horsed
Upon the sightless couriers of the air,
Shall blow the horrid deed in every eye,
That tears shall drown the wind. I have no spur
To prick the sides of my intent, but only
Vaulting ambition, which o'erleaps itself
And falls on the other –

Enter LADY MACBETH

How now, what news?

LADY MACBETH He has almost supped. Why have you left the chamber?

MACBETH Hath he asked for me?

LADY MACBETH Know you not he has? 30

MACBETH We will proceed no further in this business.
He hath honoured me of late, and I have bought
Golden opinions from all sorts of people,
Which would be worn now in their newest gloss,
Not cast aside so soon.

LADY MACBETH Was the hope drunk
Wherein you dressed yourself? Hath it slept since?
And wakes it now to look so green and pale
At what it did so freely? From this time
Such I account thy love. Art thou afeard
To be the same in thine own act and valour 40

40–1	To be . . . desire *To show the same determination in your actions and courage as you do in your desires.*
42	ornament of life *the 'golden opinions', or the crown. 'Ornament' continues the imagery of dress.*
44	wait upon *follow*
45	the . . . cat *'The cat would eat fish, and would not wet her feet' (Heywood,* Three Hundred Epigrammes).
	adage *proverb*
46	become *be fitting to*
47	is none *is not a man at all – i.e. he becomes a beast. This was a cardinal principle in the doctrine of 'order'* (see *pp 2–4): if you try to rise above your station you can only fall below it. Macbeth discovers the double truth of this when the murder of Duncan destroys both his 'humanity' and his 'manhood'. Lady Macbeth picks up his line of argument – if the murder is not manly, a beast must have suggested it.*
48	break *broach, propose*
52	Did . . . adhere *Were convenient for the enterprise*
	make both *engineer a suitable time and place. For the suggestion here of earlier plotting see pp 16–17.*
54	unmake you *destroys your manhood*
54–8	*Compare with I. 5. 47*
60	sticking-place *The notch in a cross-bow in which the cord was held after it had been wound back prior to releasing the shaft. The image might also refer to the tightening of the strings of a viol in order to tune it.*
63	chamberlains *attendants of the bed-chamber*
64	wassail *carousing*
	convince *overcome*
65	warder *The anatomy of the time placed memory in the lowest part of the brain, so it guarded the reason against deluding vapours rising from the stomach.*
66	fume *vapour*
	receipt *receptacle – the brain*
67	limbeck *alembic – a vessel used for distilling, and so filled with vapours*
68	drenched *drowned in drink, and possibly with an allusion to a medicinal 'drench' given to animals – the chamberlains are in 'swinish' sleep.*
70	put upon *ascribe to*
71	spongy *having soaked up so much wine*
72	quell *murder – from the same root as 'kill'*

As thou art in desire? Wouldst thou have that
Which thou esteem'st the ornament of life,
And live a coward in thine own esteem,
Letting 'I dare not' wait upon 'I would',
Like the poor cat i' the adage?

MACBETH Prithee, peace.
I dare do all that may become a man;
Who dares do more is none.

LADY MACBETH What beast was't then
That made you break this enterprise to me?
When you durst do it, then you were a man;
And to be more than what you were, you would 50
Be so much more the man. Nor time, nor place,
Did then adhere, and yet you would make both;
They have made themselves, and that their fitness
now
Does unmake you. I have given suck, and know
How tender 'tis to love the babe that milks me –
I would, while it was smiling in my face,
Have plucked my nipple from his boneless gums
And dashed the brains out, had I so sworn
As you have done to this.

MACBETH If we should fail?

LADY MACBETH We fail?
But screw your courage to the sticking-place, 60
And we'll not fail. When Duncan is asleep
(Whereto the rather shall his day's hard journey
Soundly invite him) his two chamberlains
Will I with wine and wassail so convince
That memory, the warder of the brain,
Shall be a fume, and the receipt of reason
A limbeck only. When in swinish sleep
Their drenchéd natures lie as in a death,
What cannot you and I perform upon
The unguardéd Duncan? What not put upon 70
His spongy officers, who shall bear the guilt
Of our great quell?

73 mettle *courage, spirit. Macbeth now accepts his wife's view of manliness.*

74 received *i.e. as true*

77 other *otherwise*

78 As we *In view of the way that we*

79–80 *Compare l. 60.*

80 corporal agent *bodily faculty.*

81 mock the time *he repeats his wife's advice (I. 5. 62–5)*

MACBETH Bring forth men-children only!
For thy undaunted mettle should compose
Nothing but males. Will it not be received,
When we have marked with blood those sleepy
two
Of his own chamber, and used their very daggers,
That they have done't?

LADY MACBETH Who dares receive it other,
As we shall make our griefs and clamour roar
Upon his death?

MACBETH I am settled, and bend up
Each corporal agent to this terrible feat. 80
Away, and mock the time with fairest show:
False face must hide what the false heart doth
know. [*Exeunt*

ACT TWO, scene 1

4 Hold *Wait*
husbandry *economy*

5 candles *the stars*
that *some other accoutrement*
6 heavy summons *call to sleep*
7 Powers *The Powers were the angelic order with the special duty of combatting demons, but the word may be used more generally here.*
8 nature *human nature. Banquo is also disturbed by the witches, and suffers from bad dreams as Macbeth does later, but unlike Macbeth he calls for spiritual aid. The extent of his agitation is shown when he demands his sword, even though he is in a friend's castle. Is there any evidence in this scene that he suspects Macbeth's intentions?*
14 largess *gifts*
offices *servants' quarters*
15–16 greets . . . hostess *acknowledges her kindness by the gift*
withal *with*
16 shut up *concluded the day*
18 Our . . . defect *The extent to which they could satisfy their desire to entertain Duncan was dependent on ('servant to') and limited by the defect of their being unprepared.*
19 free *without restrictions*
wrought *worked, operated*
All's well *everything was satisfactory*

22 can . . . serve *find a convenient time. It has been suggested that Macbeth is already using the royal plural, but 'we' probably refers to him and Banquo.*
23 would *should*
24 At . . . leisure *Whenever you should be so kind as to find the time to spare*

ACT TWO

Scene I. *Enter* BANQUO, *and* FLEANCE, *with a torch before him*

BANQUO How goes the night, boy?
FLEANCE The moon is down; I have not heard the clock.
BANQUO And she goes down at twelve.
FLEANCE I take't, 'tis later, sir.
BANQUO Hold, take my sword. There's husbandry in heaven;
Their candles are all out. Take thee that too.
A heavy summons lies like lead upon me,
And yet I would not sleep. Merciful Powers,
Restrain in me the cursèd thoughts that nature
Gives way to in repose. Give me my sword.
Enter MACBETH, *and a* SERVANT *with a torch*
Who's there? 10
MACBETH A friend.
BANQUO What, sir, not yet at rest? The king's a-bed.
He hath been in unusual pleasure, and
Sent forth great largess to your offices.
This diamond he greets your wife withal,
By the name of most kind hostess, and shut up
In measureless content.
MACBETH Being unprepared,
Our will became the servant to defect,
Which else should free have wrought.
BANQUO All's well.
I dreamt last night of the three Weird Sisters. 20
To you they have showed some truth.
MACBETH I think not of them.
Yet when we can entreat an hour to serve,
We would spend it in some words upon that business,
If you would grant the time.
BANQUO At your kind'st leisure.

25 cleave . . . consent *follow my advice – or, adhere to my party*
when 'tis *when the time is convenient – either for their discussion or for action*
26–7 so . . . it *Compare I. 7. 46–7*
28 bosom franchised *conscience free of guilt*
clear *unsullied*
29 be counselled *listen to your counsel*

31–2 *The actual purpose of the bell emerges later (ll. 62–4).*

36 fatal *portending death*
36–7 sensible to *perceptible by*

39 heat-oppressed *feverish*

41 *The short line is completed by the action of drawing his dagger.*
42 marshall'st *directs – it points towards Duncan's room*
44–5 Mine . . . rest *Either my eyes are fools compared with the other senses (if the dagger is not real) or they can detect what is hidden from all the others.*
46 dudgeon *hilt*
gouts *drops*

48–9 informs Thus *assumes this form*
49 one half-world *the hemisphere that is in darkness*
51 curtained *four-poster beds were enclosed with curtains*
51–2 Witchcraft . . . offerings *Witches make ceremonial offerings to their goddess, Hecate*
52 withered Murder *A suggestion of the morality play (see p 12).*
53 Alarumed *Called up*
54 watch *watchman's cry – the watch patrolled the streets, calling out the hour of the night.*

MACBETH If you shall cleave to my consent, when 'tis,
It shall make honour for you.

BANQUO So I lose none
In seeking to augment it, but still keep
My bosom franchised and allegiance clear,
I shall be counselled.

MACBETH Good repose the while.

BANQUO Thanks, sir; the like to you. 30

[*Exeunt* BANQUO *and* FLEANCE

MACBETH Go bid thy mistress, when my drink is ready,
She strike upon the bell. Get thee to bed.

[*Exit* SERVANT

Is this a dagger which I see before me,
The handle toward my hand? Come, let me clutch thee.
I have thee not, and yet I see thee still.
Art thou not, fatal vision, sensible
To feeling as to sight? Or art thou but
A dagger of the mind, a false creation,
Proceeding from the heat-oppressed brain?
I see thee yet, in form as palpable 40
As this which now I draw.
Thou marshall'st me the way that I was going,
And such an instrument I was to use.
Mine eyes are made the fools o' th' other senses,
Or else worth all the rest. I see thee still;
And on thy blade and dudgeon gouts of blood,
Which was not so before. – There's no such thing:
It is the bloody business which informs
Thus to mine eyes. Now o'er the one half-world
Nature seems dead, and wicked dreams abuse 50
The curtained sleep. Witchcraft celebrates
Pale Hecate's offerings; and withered Murder,
Alarumed by his sentinel, the wolf,
Whose howl's his watch, thus with his stealthy pace,

55 Tarquin *Tarquinius Sextus, whose rape of Lucretia led to the expulsion of the Tarquin kings from Rome*
design *purpose*
56 sure . . . earth *In contrast to the world of moral illusion and psychological chaos that Macbeth is entering (see p 25).*
58 prate *chatter. Kenneth Muir relates the image to* Luke, *xix. 40 and* Habakkuk, *ii. 9–12, 20.*
59 take . . . time *break the horrified silence – or, assume the same tone of horror in their outcry*
60 suits . . . it *is appropriate to the hour of murder. Throughout the speech Macbeth has been working himself into the rôle of murderer, and he concludes with a grim jingle.*

ACT TWO, scene 2

This scene follows directly on from the previous one.

1 them *the chamberlains (see I. 7 63–72). Even Lady Macbeth welcomes the courage that alcohol can give; she is clearly agitated at the beginning of the scene.*
3 bellman *Either the watchman – who rang a bell – or the bellman who preceded the corpse at a funeral. In May 1605 an endowment provided for a bellman to ring his bell before the cells of prisoners who were about to be executed in Newgate prison.*
4 stern'st good-night *grimmest farewell*
5 surfeited *i.e. with excess wine*
grooms *servants*
6 mock . . . charge *make a mockery of their duty, to guard the King*
possets *drinks of warm milk, wine, spices, etc.*
7 nature *life. Death and life are disputing over which possesses them.*
11 Confounds *Ruins*
12–13 Had . . . done't *Her first expression of natural feelings. It justifies for the audience the apparent change in her intentions (see I. 5. 51 and note).*
13 [Enter MACBETH] *How does he enter; in particular, how does he hold his hands?*
My husband! *What emotions might be expressed in this exclamation? This is the only occasion on which she speaks of Macbeth in this way.*

With Tarquin's ravishing strides, towards his
design
Moves like a ghost. Thou sure and firm-set earth,
Hear not my steps, which way they walk, for fear
Thy very stones prate of my whereabout,
And take the present horror from the time,
Which now suits with it. Whiles I threat, he
lives; 60
Words to the heat of deeds too cold breath gives.
[*A bell rings*
I go, and it is done; the bell invites me.
Hear it not, Duncan, for it is a knell
That summons thee to heaven, or to hell.
[*Exit*

Scene 2. *Enter* LADY MACBETH

LADY MACBETH That which hath made them drunk hath
made me bold;
What hath quenched them hath given me fire.
Hark! – Peace:
It was the owl that shrieked, the fatal bellman,
Which gives the stern'st good-night. He is about
it.
The doors are open; and the surfeited grooms
Do mock their charge with snores. I have drugged
their possets,
That death and nature do contend about them,
Whether they live or die.

MACBETH [*Within*] Who's there? – What, ho!

LADY MACBETH Alack, I am afraid they have awaked,
And 'tis not done! The attempt and not the deed 10
Confounds us. Hark! – I laid their daggers ready,
He could not miss 'em. Had he not resembled
My father as he slept, I had done't.
Enter MACBETH
My husband!

15 crickets *Supposed, like the owl, to presage death.*

16–19 *What is suggested by this staccato interchange? Do Macbeth and Lady Macbeth speak in the same way here?*

20 sorry *wretched*

24 addressed them to *prepared themselves for*

25 two . . . together *It has been suggested that these are Malcolm and Donalbain, but Lady Macbeth mentions only Donalbain in l. 19; and she is unlikely to refer so casually to the two chamberlains on whom she planned to lay the blame for the murder. There seems no need to identify them.*

27 As *As if*

hangman's hands *bloodstained – the hangman drew and quartered criminals as well as hanging them.*

28 Listening *Listening to*

32–3 'Amen' . . . throat *The inability to pray was a sign of demonic possession (see p 23).*

34 After *In*

so *if we do so*

make us mad *She anticipates her own fate.*

36 'Macbeth . . . sleep' *i.e. by murdering the sleeping Duncan. The prophecy will be fulfilled (see III. 2. 17–19, 4. 140, 6. 34, V. 1.). The voice may have been suggested by Holinshed's account of a similar accusing voice heard by King Kenneth after he had murdered his nephew.*

37 knits . . . sleave *smooths out the tangled skein*

38 death *Regarded here as a form of repose (compare III. 2. 22–3).*

MACBETH I have done the deed. – Didst thou not hear a noise?
LADY MACBETH I heard the owl scream, and the crickets cry.
Did not you speak?
MACBETH When?
LADY MACBETH Now.
MACBETH As I descended?
LADY MACBETH Ay.
MACBETH Hark!
Who lies i' the second chamber?
LADY MACBETH Donalbain.
MACBETH [*Looking at his hands*] This is a sorry sight. 20
LADY MACBETH A foolish thought, to say a sorry sight.
MACBETH There's one did laugh in's sleep, and one cried 'Murder!'
That they did wake each other. I stood and heard them;
But they did say their prayers, and addressed them
Again to sleep.
LADY MACBETH There are two lodged together.
MACBETH One cried 'God bless us!' and 'Amen' the other,
As they had seen me with these hangman's hands.
Listening their fear, I could not say 'Amen'
When they did say 'God bless us!'
LADY MACBETH Consider it not so deeply. 30
MACBETH But wherefore could not I pronounce 'Amen'?
I had most need of blessing, and 'Amen'
Stuck in my throat.
LADY MACBETH These deeds must not be thought
After these ways; so, it will make us mad.
MACBETH Methought I heard a voice cry 'Sleep no more!
Macbeth does murder sleep' – the innocent sleep,
Sleep that knits up the ravelled sleave of care,
The death of each day's life, sore labour's bath,

39 second course *second lap, or round – one meaning of 'course' is 'race'. The first 'course' is labour. A second meaning of 'course' as a part of a meal is picked up in the next line.*

45 unbend *Compare I. 7. 79–80.*
46 brainsickly *deliriously. Later it is she who has 'a mind diseased' (V. 3. 40).*
47 witness *evidence of the murder*
48 Why . . . place? *Did he previously conceal them, or was she too agitated to notice them?*
52 Look . . . not *Compare I. 4. 52–3.*
53–4 The sleeping . . . pictures *Similar in being like pictures of the living, or conscious, person. The resemblance of sleep to death is a common idea in the play (see II. 2. 7–8, 38, 3. 75–6, III. 2. 22–3) and contributes to the theme of false appearances (see p 25).*
55 painted devil *A picture, or an actor made up as the devil – another recollection of the morality plays*
56–7 gild . . . guilt *A sardonic pun – does it express callousness or tension?*
57 [Knocking within] *For the dramatic effect of the knocking on the gate see pp 19–20.*
59 What . . . eyes *Compare I. 4. 52. R. Walker relates this line to* Matthew, *xviii. 9 and* Luke, *xi. 34–6, and Kenneth Muir has pointed out that the former chapter also mentions hell fire, and the latter Beelzebub and knocking, all of which may have contributed to the beginning of the next scene. See also* Matthew, *vi. 22, 23.*
62 incarnadine *dye blood-red. There are similar images in Seneca's tragedies* Phaedra *and* Hercules Furens.
63 green . . . red *The previous rolling, polysyllabic line is condensed into curt monosyllables. Some editors make 'one' qualify 'red' ('totally red'), but a comma after 'one' in the Folio indicates that it is the 'green one' (the sea) that is turned red.*

Balm of hurt minds, great nature's second course,
Chief nourisher in life's feast, –

LADY MACBETH What do you mean? 40

MACBETH Still it cried 'Sleep no more!' to all the house;
'Glamis hath murdered sleep, and therefore Cawdor
Shall sleep no more; Macbeth shall sleep no more'.

LADY MACBETH Who was it that thus cried? Why, worthy Thane,
You do unbend your noble strength to think
So brainsickly of things. Go get some water,
And wash this filthy witness from your hand.
Why did you bring these daggers from the place?
They must lie there. Go, carry them, and smear
The sleepy grooms with blood.

MACBETH I'll go no more: 50
I am afraid to think what I have done;
Look on't again I dare not.

LADY MACBETH Infirm of purpose!
Give me the daggers. The sleeping and the dead
Are but as pictures; 'tis the eye of childhood
That fears a painted devil. If he do bleed,
I'll gild the faces of the grooms withal.
For it must seem their guilt.

[*Exit. Knocking within*

MACBETH Whence is that knocking?
How is't with me, when every noise appals me?
What hands are here? Ha! they pluck out mine eyes.
Will all great Neptune's ocean wash this blood 60
Clean from my hand? No, this my hand will rather
The multitudinous seas incarnadine,
Making the green one red.

Enter LADY MACBETH

68–9 Your ... unattended *Your firmness of purpose has deserted you.*
70 nightgown *dressing gown*
occasion *circumstances*
71 watchers *still awake*
72 poorly *weakly*
73 To know ... myself *He means 'I would sooner not know myself than have to recognise what I have done', but his words have a further possible meaning – 'In order to contemplate what I have done I need to forget my real self'.*

ACT TWO, scene 3

This scene is connected even more closely with the previous one by the continued knocking, which becomes louder as we move into the open air and the knockers become more impatient. For the significance of the Porter's speeches see pp 14–15.

2 old *plenty of*
4 Belzebub *Beelzebub, one of the chief devils.*
4–5 hanged ... plenty *He had hoarded grain, expecting the price to rise, but a plentiful harvest would make it drop and he would be ruined. There were good harvests in 1605 and 1606, but the joke was an old one.*
5–6 time-server *Someone who ingratiates himself by adapting his opinions and behaviour to those current at the time (compare I. 5. 62–3). Dover Wilson suggested this emendation of the Folio's 'Come in time' ('Come in good time') so that the phrase would be parallel to those addressed to the equivocator and the tailor. He points out that all farmers 'serve time' by complying with the changes in the seasons, and that as 'server' also means 'waiter' it explains the link with 'napkins'.*
6 napkins enow *enough handkerchiefs*
8 equivocator *See pp 1–2. Garnet used 'Farmer' as a pseudonym.*
9 swear ... scale *His declarations on oath were so ambiguous that he could maintain that he meant either of two contradictory things. The 'scales' are those of justice.*
13–14 stealing ... hose *French hose were tightly fitting breeches, with no cloth to spare, so he over-reached himself when he tried to steal some of the material.*
15 roast ... goose *heat your smoothing iron*
18–19 primrose ... bonfire *the path of pleasure that leads to hell*

LADY MACBETH My hands are of your colour; but I shame
To wear a heart so white. [*Knocking*] I hear a knocking
At the south entry. Retire we to our chamber.
A little water clears us of this deed;
How easy is it then! Your constancy
Hath left you unattended. [*Knocking*] Hark, more knocking.
Get on your nightgown, lest occasion call us 70
And show us to be watchers. Be not lost
So poorly in your thoughts.

MACBETH To know my deed, 'twere best not know myself. [*Knocking*
Wake Duncan with thy knocking! I would thou couldst. [*Exeunt*

Scene 3. *Knocking within. Enter a* PORTER

PORTER Here's a knocking indeed! If a man were porter of hell-gate, he should have old turning the key. [*Knocking*] Knock, knock, knock. Who's there, i' th' name of Belzebub? Here's a farmer, that hanged himself on the expectation of plenty. Come in time-server; have napkins enow about you, here you'll sweat for't. [*Knocking*] Knock, knock. Who's there, i' th' other devil's name? Faith, here's an equivocator, that could swear in both the scales against either scale; who committed treason enough for God's sake, yet 10 could not equivocate to heaven. O, come in, equivocator. [*Knocking*] Knock, knock, knock. Who's there? Faith, here's an English tailor come hither for stealing out of a French hose. Come in, tailor, here you may roast your goose. [*Knocking*] Knock, knock. Never at quiet! What are you? But this place is too cold for hell. I'll devil-porter it no further. I had thought to have let in some of all professions that go the primrose way

20 remember the porter *i.e. with a tip*

23–4 second cock *literally, the second cockcrow – about 3 a.m.*

27 nose-painting *it reddens the nose*
27–35 *For the relation of this discourse to Macbeth see pp 14–15. His ambition has already been compared to drunkenness (I. 7. 35–6) and murder to lechery (II. 1. 55), and the barrenness of his achievement is later represented in terms of sexual sterility (see pp 28–9).*
28 provokes . . . unprovokes *stimulates and inhibits*
31 makes . . . mars him *increases his feelings of potency and manhood, while in fact reducing them (compare I. 7. 46–7)*
31–2 sets . . . off *encourages him, while making him impotent*
33 stand to *In addition to the obscene allusion, 'stand to' means 'affirm the truth of', leading on to the reference to equivocation in the next line.*
34 equivocates . . . sleep *deceives him with a dream*
35 giving . . . lie *declaring that he lies (because he is unable to do what he said he would), and also 'throws him down', which introduces the allusions to wrestling in the next speech ('throat', 'strong', 'took up my legs', 'cast').*
37 i'the . . . throat *A 'lie in the throat' was a direct lie, unlike equivocation.*
on *of*
38 requited . . . lie *repaid him for the accusation of lying*
40 made a shift *contrived*
cast *throw, with the additional suggestion of 'throw up', vomit*
45 timely *early*
46 slipped the hour *missed the time*

48 'tis one *i.e. a trouble*
49 physics pain *itself cures the pains we take over it (compare I. 4. 44). Macbeth conceals his real feelings by quoting a proverbial expression.*

to th' everlasting bonfire. [*Knocking*] Anon, anon! I pray you, remember the porter. [*Opens the gate* 20

Enter MACDUFF *and* LENNOX

MACDUFF Was it so late, friend, ere you went to bed,
That you do lie so late?

PORTER Faith, sir, we were carousing till the second cock; and drink, sir, is a great provoker of three things.

MACDUFF What three things does drink especially provoke?

PORTER Marry, sir, nose-painting, sleep, and urine. Lechery, sir, it provokes, and unprovokes: it provokes the desire, but it takes away the performance. Therefore much drink may be said to be an equivocator 30 with lechery: it makes him, and it mars him; it sets him on, and it takes him off; it persuades him, and disheartens him; makes him stand to, and not stand to; in conclusion, equivocates him in a sleep, and, giving him the lie, leaves him.

MACDUFF I believe drink gave thee the lie last night.

PORTER That it did, sir, i' the very throat on me; but I requited him for his lie, and, I think, being too strong for him, though he took up my legs sometime, yet I made a shift to cast him. 40

MACDUFF Is thy master stirring?

Enter MACBETH

Our knocking has awaked him; here he comes.

LENNOX Good morrow, noble sir.

MACBETH Good morrow, both.

MACDUFF Is the King stirring, worthy Thane?

MACBETH Not yet.

MACDUFF He did command me to call timely on him;
I have almost slipped the hour.

MACBETH I'll bring you to him.

MACDUFF I know this is a joyful trouble to you;
But yet 'tis one.

MACBETH The labour we delight in physics pain.
This is the door.

51 limited *appointed*

52 appoint *arrange. The change to the past tense is significant.*

53–60 *The storm is a reflection in the natural world of the disorder in the kingdom (see pp 2–3, and introductory note to II. 4.). There may be an allusion to the hurricane of 29–30 March, 1606.*

57 dire combustion *disastrous civil conflagration – perhaps with an allusion to the Gunpowder Plot.*

58 New . . . time *The unhappy time (already plagued with insurrection) has given birth to new disorders*

obscure bird *bird of darkness, the owl. Some editors substitute a comma for the Folio's full-stop after 'time', so that it is the owl that is prophesying – 'hatched' might justify this.*

60 feverous . . . shake *A common explanation of earthquakes at the time. The metaphor links the natural world with human disorders. Compare also II. 1. 56–60.*

'Twas a rough night *Is Macbeth learning to assume his wife's nonchalance, or is this, and the brevity of his other replies, a sign of nervousness?*

61 young remembrance *youthful memory*

61–2 parallel . . . it *recall another like it*

65 Confusion *Chaos, utter ruin*

66–7 sacrilegious . . . temple *See p 2. The 'Lord's anointed temple' is Duncan's body, anointed with oil at his coronation. The image combines St Paul's description of the Christian as 'the temple of the living God' (2* Corinthians, *vi. 16 with David's sparing of Saul because he was the Lord's anointed (1* Samuel, *xxiv. 10), and there may be another echo of* Habakkuk, *ii. 20 – see note to II. 1. 58.*

68–9 What . . . Majesty *They speak together.*

71 Gorgon *Medusa, the monster in Greek mythology who turned anyone who looked at her to stone – petrified him.*

MACDUFF I'll make so bold to call, 50
For 'tis my limited service.

[*Exit*

LENNOX Goes the King hence today?

MACBETH He does; he did appoint so.

LENNOX The night has been unruly. Where we lay,
Our chimneys were blown down, and, as they say,
Lamentings heard i' th' air; strange screams of death,
And prophesying, with accents terrible,
Of dire combustion, and confused events
New hatched to the woeful time. The obscure bird
Clamoured the livelong night. Some say the earth
Was feverous, and did shake.

MACBETH 'Twas a rough night. 60

LENNOX My young remembrance cannot parallel
A fellow to it.

Enter MACDUFF

MACDUFF O horror, horror, horror!
Tongue nor heart cannot conceive nor name thee.

MACBETH, LENNOX What's the matter?

MACDUFF Confusion now hath made his masterpiece!
Most sacrilegious murder hath broke ope
The Lord's anointed temple, and stole thence
The life o' the building!

MACBETH What is't you say – the life?

LENNOX Mean you his Majesty?

MACDUFF Approach the chamber, and destroy your sight 70
With a new Gorgon. Do not bid me speak;
See, and then speak yourselves.

[*Exeunt* MACBETH *and* LENNOX

Awake, awake!
Ring the alarum-bell. Murder and treason!

75 counterfeit *imitation. See II. 2. 53–4 and note.*

77 great . . . image *picture of the Judgement Day, which it resembles in its horror, if not in its divine justice*

78 As . . . sprites *As the souls of the dead will rise on Judgement Day*

79 countenance *Combines the two meanings of 'suit with' and 'behold'. In the Folio the line continues with 'Ring the bell', but as it is completed metrically by Lady Macbeth's first words this was probably a stage direction which was incorporated into the text by error.*

[Bell rings] *the heavy alarm bell of the castle, which would toll confusedly for some time, adding to the turmoil.*

80 parley *discussion between opposing forces in a battle. For Macbeth the bell sounds like a trumpet summoning a parley.*

83 repetition *recital*

86 What . . . house? *A difficult line for the actress; is it inept or cunning?*

Too . . . anywhere *Is this a rebuke?*

89 chance *unexpected misfortune*

91 serious *of consequence*

mortality *mortal life*

92 toys *triviality*

93 drawn *drawn off*

lees *dregs*

94 vault *the earth, vaulted over by the sky – with the suggestion of both a wine vault and a burial vault*

96 head *fountain head*

98 O . . . whom? *Another apparently difficult line, but a natural enough response if, as appears later, Malcolm and Donalbain immediately fear for themselves. Through the rest of the scene they stand apart, watching suspiciously.*

Banquo and Donalbain! Malcolm, awake!
Shake off this downy sleep, death's counterfeit,
And look on death itself! Up, up, and see
The great doom's image! Malcolm! Banquo!
As from your graves rise up, and walk like sprites,
To countenance this horror!

[*Bell rings*

Enter LADY MACBETH

LADY MACBETH What's the business,
That such a hideous trumpet calls to parley 80
The sleepers of the house? Speak, speak!

MACDUFF O gentle lady,
'Tis not for you to hear what I can speak:
The repetition in a woman's ear
Would murder as it fell.

Enter BANQUO

O Banquo, Banquo,
Our royal master's murdered!

LADY MACBETH Woe, alas!
What! in our house?

BANQUO Too cruel anywhere.
Dear Duff, I prithee contradict thyself,
And say it is not so.

Enter MACBETH *and* LENNOX

MACBETH Had I but died an hour before this chance,
I had lived a blessed time; for, from this instant, 90
There's nothing serious in mortality;
All is but toys. Renown and grace is dead,
The wine of life is drawn, and the mere lees
Is left this vault to brag of.

Enter MALCOLM *and* DONALBAIN

DONALBAIN What is amiss?

MACBETH You are, and do not know't.
The spring, the head, the fountain of your blood,
Is stopped; the very source of it is stopped.

MACDUFF Your royal father's murdered.

MALCOLM O! by whom?

100 badged *wearing the badge of their trade (see l. 113)*

102 They . . . distracted *Perhaps the after-effects of Lady Macbeth's drug.*

105 Wherefore . . . so? *Is he suspicious?*

106 amazed *bewildered*

108 expedition *haste, impetuosity*

109 pauser *that which makes one pause and think*

110 laced *striped, or embroidered – as if with golden thread (compare II. 2. 56–7)*

111 breach in nature *as if nature itself had been wounded by the death of the King*

112 wasteful *laying waste, like an army after it has entered the breach in a city wall*

113 colours . . . trade *livery worn by members of a trade guild – in this case blood*

114 Unmannerly breeched *Indecently clothed. The strained imagery of this speech, which continues the theme of clothing ('laced', 'breeched'), perhaps reflects the strain on Macbeth.*

116 Help me hence *Her fainting may be genuine, or feigned to cause a diversion because she fears that her husband is being carried away and is overplaying his part.*

118–19 that . . . ours *who might claim most interest in the subject being discussed*

120 in an auger-hole *i.e. in something as insignificant as a hole bored with an auger – and also with an allusion to the hole made by a dagger*

122 brewed *ready to be poured out*

123 Upon . . . motion *Ready to express itself (perhaps in action as well as words)*

LENNOX Those of his chamber, as it seemed, had done't:
Their hands and faces were all badged with blood; 100
So were their daggers, which unwiped we found
Upon their pillow. They stared, and were distracted;
No man's life was to be trusted with them.

MACBETH O yet I do repent me of my fury,
That I did kill them.

MACDUFF Wherefore did you so?

MACBETH Who can be wise, amazed, temperate and furious,
Loyal and neutral, in a moment? No man.
The expedition of my violent love
Outrun the pauser, reason. Here lay Duncan,
His silver skin laced with his golden blood, 110
And his gashed stabs looked like a breach in nature
For ruin's wasteful entrance; there, the murderers,
Steeped in the colours of their trade, their daggers
Unmannerly breeched with gore. Who could refrain,
That had a heart to love, and in that heart
Courage to make 's love known?

LADY MACBETH Help me hence, ho!

MACDUFF Look to the lady.

MALCOLM [*Aside to* DONALBAIN] Why do we hold our tongues, that most may claim
This argument for ours?

DONALBAIN [*Aside to* MALCOLM] What should be spoken
Here, where our fate, hid in an auger-hole, 120
May rush and seize us? Let's away;
Our tears are not yet brewed.

MALCOLM [*Aside to* DONALBAIN] Nor our strong sorrow
Upon the foot of motion.

BANQUO Look to the lady.

124 naked . . . hid *covered our ill-clad, shivering bodies*

126 question *inquire into*
127 scruples *doubts*

129 undivulged pretence *undisclosed intention*

131 briefly *quickly*
133 consort *mix*
134 office *duty. He may have Macbeth in mind as he has been most voluble in his sorrow.*
138–9 the near . . . bloody *the closer one's relationship to the King, the more likely one is to be murdered*
139 shaft *arrow*
140 lighted *returned to earth, or hit its mark*
142 dainty *particular about the courtesies*
143 shift *slip*
warrant *justification*
theft *of oneself – punning on 'steal away'*

ACT TWO, scene 4

This scene rounds off the first part of the play by filling in the plot and making explicit the most important characteristic of the murder, its unnaturalness (see ll. 10, 27 and pp 2–3, 27–8). Many of the unnatural events referred to – and perhaps the storm described in II. 3. – are taken from Holinshed's account of the murder of King Duff:

> *For the space of six moneths togither . . . there appeered no sunne by day, nor moone by night in anie part of the realme, but still was the skie covered with continuall clouds, and sometimes such outragious windes arose, with lightenings and tempests, that the people were in great feare of present destruction . . . horsses in Louthian, being of singular beautie and swiftnesse, did eate their owne flesh . . . There was a sparhawke also strangled by an owle.*

3 sore *grievous*

LADY MACBETH is carried out

And when we have our naked frailties hid,
That suffer in exposure, let us meet
And question this most bloody piece of work,
To know it further. Fears and scruples shake us.
In the great hand of God I stand, and thence
Against the undivulged pretence I fight
Of treasonous malice.

MACDUFF And so do I.

ALL So all. 130

MACBETH Let's briefly put on manly readiness,
And meet i' the hall together.

ALL Well contented.

Exeunt all but MALCOLM and DONALBAIN

MALCOLM What will you do? Let's not consort with them.
To show an unfelt sorrow is an office
Which the false man does easy. I'll to England.

DONALBAIN To Ireland, I: our separated fortune
Shall keep us both the safer. Where we are
There's daggers in men's smiles – the near in blood,
The nearer bloody.

MALCOLM This murderous shaft that's shot
Hath not yet lighted, and our safest way 140
Is to avoid the aim. Therefore to horse;
And let us not be dainty of leave-taking,
But shift away. There's warrant in that theft
Which steals itself, when there's no mercy left.

[*Exeunt*

Scene 4. *Enter ROSS and an OLD MAN*

OLD MAN Threescore and ten I can remember well,
Within the volume of which time I have seen
Hours dreadful, and things strange; but this sore night

4 trifled . . . knowings *made previous experience seem trivial*

6 bloody stage *the earth, scene of bloody deeds. The image of the stage has been anticipated by 'act' and also by 'heavens' – the name given to the canopy, painted with the signs of the zodiac, that extended over the stage.*
7 travelling lamp *the sun, travelling across the sky*
8 predominance *predominant astrological influence*
the day's shame *the day hiding with shame*

12 towering . . . place *Technical terms in falconry – circling upwards to the highest pitch of its flight.*
13 mousing *that catches mice*

15 minions *favourites*
race *breed*
16 in nature *in their natures*
17 Contending . . . obedience *Rebelling against the obedience they owe to man.*

23 Those . . . slain *Probably ironic, but Ross does not perceive it.*
24 good *i.e. to themselves*
pretend *intend*
suborned *bribed*

Hath trifled former knowings.

ROSS Ha, good father,
Thou seest the heavens, as troubled with man's act,
Threaten his bloody stage. By the clock 'tis day,
And yet dark night strangles the travelling lamp.
Is't night's predominance, or the day's shame,
That darkness does the face of earth entomb
When living light should kiss it?

OLD MAN 'Tis unnatural, 10
Even like the deed that's done. On Tuesday last,
A falcon, towering in her pride of place,
Was by a mousing owl hawked at and killed.

ROSS And Duncan's horses – a thing most strange and certain –
Beauteous and swift, the minions of their race,
Turned wild in nature, broke their stalls, flung out,
Contending 'gainst obedience, as they would make
War with mankind.

OLD MAN 'Tis said they eat each other.

ROSS They did so, to the amazement of mine eyes
That looked upon't.
Here comes the good Macduff. 20

Enter MACDUFF

How goes the world, sir, now?

MACDUFF Why, see you not?

ROSS Is't known who did this more than bloody deed?

MACDUFF Those that Macbeth hath slain.

ROSS Alas the day,
What good could they pretend?

MACDUFF They were suborned.
Malcolm and Donalbain, the King's two sons,
Are stol'n away and fled, which puts upon them
Suspicion of the deed.

27 still *again*

28 Thriftless *Wasteful*
ravin up *devour savagely*

29 Thine . . . means *The source of your own life.*

31 named *elected*
Scone *The ancient capital of Scotland.*

33 Colme-kill *Iona, the island of St Columba, where the Scottish kings were buried.*

36 Fife *His own castle.*
thither *i.e. to Scone*

37 Well . . . there *Kenneth Muir points out that Macduff picks up Ross's 'Well' ironically.*

38 Lest . . . new *The first explicit, if veiled, criticism of Macbeth. The image from clothing is suggested here by the robes worn at the investiture.*

40 benison *blessing*

ROSS 'Gainst nature still;
Thriftless ambition, that will ravin up
Thine own life's means! Then 'tis most like
The sovereignty will fall upon Macbeth. 30

MACDUFF He is already named, and gone to Scone
To be invested.

ROSS Where is Duncan's body?

MACDUFF Carried to Colme-kill,
The sacred storehouse of his predecessors,
And guardian of their bones.

ROSS Will you to Scone?

MACDUFF No cousin, I'll to Fife.

ROSS Well, I will thither.

MACDUFF Well, may you see things well done there –
Adieu –
Lest our old robes sit easier than our new!

ROSS Farewell, father.

OLD MAN God's benison go with you, and with those 40
That would make good of bad, and friends of foes.

[*Exeunt*

ACT THREE, scene I

Banquo's soliloquy opens the second part of the play, concerned with his murder. It is closely linked with the previous scene, which concluded with Macduff's doubts about Macbeth; this begins with Banquo's certainty of his guilt.

4 stand . . . posterity *remain with your descendents*
5–6 root . . . kings *See pp 7–8.*

7 shine *i.e. with the light of truth and the brilliance of his good fortune*
8 verities . . . good *truths that have been demonstrated with regard to you*
9 oracles *predictions*
10 [Sennet] *A ceremonial flourish on a trumpet or cornet. Macbeth's entrance is formal and stately.*

12 gap . . . feast *She is gracious, but condescending – she does not address Banquo directly – and there may be a veiled menace in her words: the feast* they *hope to enjoy would be ruined if they forgot to deal with Banquo.*
13 all-thing unbecoming *altogether inappropriate*
14 solemn *ceremonial*
16 the which *i.e. command. Banquo's cold politeness contrasts with his earlier easy friendship with Macbeth and with the warmth of his professions of loyalty to Duncan.*

20 else *otherwise*
21 still *always*
grave *weighty*
prosperous *profitable*
22 we'll . . . tomorrow *use tomorrow for the same purpose*
23 Is't . . . ride? *Macbeth adopts a regal dignity of phrase now that he is king, but these apparently casual questions about Banquo's riding have a pointed brevity.*
25 this *now*
the better *faster than I expect*

ACT THREE

Scene I. *Enter* BANQUO

BANQUO Thou hast it now, King, Cawdor, Glamis, all,
As the weird women promised, and I fear
Thou play'dst most foully for't; yet it was said
It should not stand in thy posterity,
But that myself should be the root and father
Of many kings. If there come truth from them,
As upon thee, Macbeth, their speeches shine,
Why, by the verities on thee made good,
May they not be my oracles as well,
And set me up in hope? But hush, no more. 10

Sennet sounded. Enter MACBETH *as King,* LADY MACBETH *as Queen,* LENNOX, ROSS, LORDS, *and* ATTENDANTS

MACBETH Here's our chief guest.
LADY MACBETH If he had been forgotten,
It had been as a gap in our great feast,
And all-thing unbecoming.
MACBETH Tonight we hold a solemn supper, sir,
And I'll request your presence.
BANQUO Let your Highness
Command upon me, to the which my duties
Are with a most indissoluble tie
For ever knit.
MACBETH Ride you this afternoon?
BANQUO Ay, my good lord.
MACBETH We should have else desired your good advice, 20
Which still hath been both grave and prosperous,
In this day's council; but we'll take tomorrow.
Is't far you ride?
BANQUO As far, my lord, as will fill up the time
'Twixt this and supper. Go not my horse the better,

26–7 become . . . twain *use one or two hours of darkness – to complete the ride*
27 Fail . . . feast *It is ironical that Banquo's obedience to this command (pointed by ll. 15–18 above) initiates Macbeth's downfall (see III. 4. 40–120).*
29 bloody cousins *murderous kinsmen*
bestowed *settled*

32 strange invention *fantastic stories – doubtless accusing him of the murder*
33 therewithal *in addition*
cause *affairs*
34 Craving us jointly *Demanding the attention of both of us*
36 our . . . upon's *it is time for us to go*

38 commend *entrust – another ironic jest, in the guise of a polite farewell*

40 master . . . time *employ the time as he wishes*

42 The . . . welcome *More welcome (to me).*
43 While *Until.*

44 Sirrah *A term used to address inferiors.*
44–5 Attend . . . pleasure? *Are they waiting for me to be ready to see them?*

47 thus *as I am now – a king, but insecure*
48 But . . . thus *implying, that is what matters*
49 Stick deep *i.e. like daggers*
royalty of nature *natural regality – he recognises that Banquo is better fitted to be king.*
50 would *should*
51 to *added to*
temper *quality*

55 Genius *Guardian spirit.*
rebuked *cowed*

I must become a borrower of the night
For a dark hour or twain.

MACBETH Fail not our feast.

BANQUO My lord, I will not.

MACBETH We hear our bloody cousins are bestowed
In England and in Ireland, not confessing 30
Their cruel parricide, filling their hearers
With strange invention; but of that tomorrow,
When therewithal we shall have cause of state
Craving us jointly. Hie you to horse; adieu,
Till you return at night. Goes Fleance with you?

BANQUO Ay, my good lord; our time does call upon's.

MACBETH I wish your horses swift and sure of foot;
And so I do commend you to their backs.
Farewell.

[*Exit Banquo*

Let every man be master of his time 40
Till seven at night; to make society
The sweeter welcome, we will keep ourself
Till supper-time alone. While then, God be with
you.

[*Exeunt all except* MACBETH *and an* ATTENDANT

Sirrah, a word with you. Attend those men
Our pleasure?

ATTENDANT They are, my lord, without the palace gate.

MACBETH Bring them before us.

[*Exit* ATTENDANT

To be thus is nothing,
But to be safely thus. Our fears in Banquo
Stick deep; and in his royalty of nature
Reigns that which would be feared. 'Tis much he
dares, 50
And, to that dauntless temper of his mind,
He hath a wisdom that doth guide his valour
To act in safety. There is none but he
Whose being I do fear; and under him
My Genius is rebuked, as it is said

55–6 as . . . Caesar *Plutarch records this of Antony and Octavius Caesar. Shakespeare refers to it again in his next tragedy,* Antony and Cleopatra.

56 chid *rebuked*

60 fruitless *barren – without offspring*

61 gripe *grip*

62 with *by*

unlineal *not in my line of descent*

63 No . . . succeeding *The witches did not actually say this.*

64 issue *offspring*

filed *defiled*

66 rancours *bitterness*

vessel . . . peace *This image may have been suggested by the Biblical image of a man's lot as a cup that must be drunk* (Psalms, *xi. 6,* Isaiah, *li. 17,* Luke, *xxii. 42*), *and by the communion cup – a 'vessel of reconciliation'. It recalls the 'poisoned chalice' (I. 7. 11) and anticipates Macbeth's attempt to drink Banquo's health (III. 4. 88–9) when his peace is destroyed by Banquo's ghost.*

67 eternal jewel *immortal soul*

68 common . . . man *i.e. Satan*

70 fate *Macbeth is defying fate in trying to frustrate the witches' prophecies about Banquo.*

list *the lists in a tournament, the field*

71 champion *challenge, fight with me*

utterance *uttermost, death*

Who's there *The common formula for summoning a servant.*

76 he *i.e. Banquo*

77 under fortune *beneath the good fortune you deserved*

78 made good *demonstrated*

79 passed in probation *went over the proofs; or the phrase may qualify 'conference' – the conference that was occupied by my proving it to you*

80 borne in hand *deceived, 'led up the garden path'*

crossed *thwarted*

the instruments *the means used*

81 Who . . . them *The agents who used them*

82 half a soul *a half wit*

notion *mind*

83 You . . . us *Gruffly noncommittal – he isn't interested in this elaborate justification.*

Mark Antony's was by Caesar. He chid the sisters
When first they put the name of king upon me,
And bade them speak to him. Then, prophet-like,
They hailed him father to a line of kings.
Upon my head they placed a fruitless crown, 60
And put a barren sceptre in my gripe,
Thence to be wrenched with an unlineal hand,
No son of mine succeeding. If't be so,
For Banquo's issue have I filed my mind,
For them the gracious Duncan have I murdered,
Put rancours in the vessel of my peace
Only for them, and mine eternal jewel
Given to the common enemy of man,
To make them kings, the seed of Banquo kings!
Rather than so, come, fate, into the list, 70
And champion me to the utterance. Who's there?

Re-enter ATTENDANT, *with two* MURDERERS

Now go to the door, and stay there till we call.

[*Exit* ATTENDANT

Was it not yesterday we spoke together?

FIRST MURDERER It was, so please your Highness.

MACBETH Well then, now
Have you considered of my speeches? Know
That it was he in the times past which held you
So under fortune, which you thought had been
Our innocent self. This I made good to you
In our last conference, passed in probation with you –
How you were borne in hand, how crossed, the instruments, 80
Who wrought with them, and all things else that might
To half a soul and to a notion crazed
Say 'Thus did Banquo'.

FIRST MURDERER You made it known to us.

85 Our point *The point of our*

87 let . . . go *ignore it*
gospelled *soaked in the Gospels – in particular,* Matthew v. *44: 'Love your enemies . . . pray for them which despitefully use you'.*
88 issue *offspring*
90 yours *i.e. your offspring*
We . . . men *An echo of Macbeth's protest to his wife (I. 7. 46–7). It initiates a further consideration of the nature of manhood.*
91 in . . . men *you are classified under the general name of 'men'*
93 Shoughs *Shaggy dogs*
water-rugs *rough-haired water-dogs*
demi-wolves *cross-breeds, half wolf*
clept *called*
94 valued file *the list that shows their individual qualities and value*
96 housekeeper *watchdog*
98 closed *enclosed*
99 Particular addition *The addition of their particular qualities*
from *as distinct from*
99–100 bill . . . alike *the list in which they are all entered merely as 'dogs'*
100 and so of men *Macbeth's stress on the due ordering of dogs and men, as determined by 'bounteous nature', is highly ironic in view of his own violation of the natural ordering of human society.*
101 station *appointed place*
file *list, or military file – the second meaning is suggested by 'rank' in the next line*
103–4 put . . . off *tell you a project, to be kept secret, the execution of which will dispose of your enemy*
105 Grapples *Binds*
106 Who . . . life *Whose life is precarious while he lives – combining the imagery of disease and clothes.*
107 Which . . . perfect *But who would be made perfectly sound by his death*
111 tugged *dragged about*
112 set . . . chance *risk my life for any opportunity*

MACBETH I did so; and went further, which is now
Our point of second meeting. Do you find
Your patience so predominant in your nature
That you can let this go? Are you so gospelled
To pray for this good man, and for his issue,
Whose heavy hand hath bowed you to the grave,
And beggared yours for ever?

FIRST MURDERER We are men, my liege. 90

MACBETH Ay, in the catalogue ye go for men;
As hounds, and greyhounds, mongrels, spaniels, curs,
Shoughs, water-rugs, and demi-wolves are clept
All by the name of dogs. The valued file
Distinguishes the swift, the slow, the subtle,
The housekeeper, the hunter, every one
According to the gift which bounteous nature
Hath in him closed, whereby he does receive
Particular addition from the bill
That writes them all alike; and so of men. 100
Now, if you have a station in the file,
Not i' the worst rank of manhood, say't,
And I will put that business in your bosoms
Whose execution takes your enemy off,
Grapples you to the heart and love of us,
Who wear our health but sickly in his life,
Which in his death were perfect.

SECOND MURDERER I am one, my liege,
Whom the vile blows and buffets of the world
Have so incensed that I am reckless what
I do to spite the world.

FIRST MURDERER And I another, 110
So weary with disasters, tugged with fortune,
That I would set my life on any chance,
To mend it or be rid on't.

MACBETH Both of you
Know Banquo was your enemy.

BOTH MURDERERS True, my lord.

115 distance *A technical term for the space between two fencers – Banquo is so dangerously close to him.*

116–17 thrusts . . . life *is an immediate threat to my life*

119 bid . . . it *justify it by no other reason than that it was my wish*

120 For *Because of*

121 Whose . . . drop *Whose affection I must not lose*

but . . . fall *but instead must lament his death*

123 to . . . love *make advances to you for assistance*

124 common *public*

127 Your . . . you *Your courage is evident. (He has no time for the murderer's heroics.)*

129 perfect . . . time *exact information about the time to do it (?) – a phrase that has baffled commentators*

130 on't *of it*

131 something from *at some distance from*

131–2 always . . . clearness *always bearing in mind that I want a clean job, leaving my reputation unsullied*

133 rubs *roughnesses, imperfections*

botches *bunglings*

135 absence *disappearance*

material *important*

137 Resolve . . . apart *Make up your minds in private*

138 anon *immediately*

139 straight *straight away*

140–1 *Compare II. 1. 63–4.*

MACBETH So is he mine; and in such bloody distance
That every minute of his being thrusts
Against my near'st of life; and though I could
With barefaced power sweep him from my sight,
And bid my will avouch it, yet I must not,
For certain friends that are both his and mine, 120
Whose loves I may not drop, but wail his fall
Who I myself struck down. And thence it is
That I to your assistance do make love,
Masking the business from the common eye
For sundry weighty reasons.

SECOND MURDERER We shall, my lord,
Perform what you command us.

FIRST MURDERER Though our lives –

MACBETH Your spirits shine through you. Within this hour, at most,
I will advise you where to plant yourselves,
Acquaint you with the perfect spy o' the time,
The moment on 't, for 't must be done tonight, 130
And something from the palace; always thought
That I require a clearness – and with him,
To leave no rubs nor botches in the work,
Fleance his son, that keeps him company,
Whose absence is no less material to me
Than is his father's, must embrace the fate
Of that dark hour. Resolve yourselves apart;
I'll come to you anon.

BOTH MURDERERS We are resolved, my lord.

MACBETH I'll call upon you straight; abide within.
[*Exeunt* MURDERERS
It is concluded. Banquo, thy soul's flight, 140
If it find heaven, must find it out tonight.
[*Exit*

ACT THREE, scene 2

1 *Her suspicions may have been aroused by Macbeth's questioning of Banquo.*

3 I . . . leisure *I am waiting until he is at leisure*

4–5 Nought's . . . content *Nothing is gained, everything is wasted, when we get what we desire but it does not bring us peace of mind.*

7 doubtful *uncertain, full of doubts and suspicions*

8 keep alone *His guilt separates him even from his partner in crime.*

9 sorriest *most miserable. She rebukes him for what she has been doing herself; there is a marked similarity in their disillusionment.*

10 Using *Keeping company with*

12 without regard *ignored*

what's . . . done *Compare I. 7. 1–2.*

13 scorched *slashed, wounded. The word means the same as 'scotched', which is often substituted for it.*

14 close *heal*

poor malice *ineffectual enmity*

15 former tooth *the power she had before to harm us*

16 frame of things *structure of the universe*

disjoint *fall to pieces*

both the worlds *earth and heaven*

20 our peace *our peace of mind, by satisfying our ambition*

to peace *to the peace of death*

21 on . . . lie *The metaphor suggests the rack.*

22 ecstasy *the state of 'being beside oneself' – here, from fear. At the time this was understood literally as the separation of the soul from the body. See I. 3. 57.*

23 fitful *full of fits – spasmodic, purposeless bursts of energy. Macbeth already approaches the complete disillusionment that he feels at the end of the play (V. 5. 19–28). and sees his own 'disease' as infecting the whole of life.*

25 Malice domestic *hostility in his own kingdom*

foreign levy *armies levied abroad*

Scene 2. *Enter* LADY MACBETH *and a* SERVANT

LADY MACBETH Is Banquo gone from Court?
SERVANT Ay, madam, but returns again tonight.
LADY MACBETH Say to the King, I would attend his leisure
For a few words.
SERVANT Madam, I will. [*Exit*
LADY MACBETH Nought's had, all's spent,
Where our desire is got without content.
'Tis safer to be that which we destroy
Than by destruction dwell in doubtful joy.

Enter MACBETH

How now, my lord? Why do you keep alone,
Of sorriest fancies your companions making,
Using those thoughts which should indeed have died 10
With them they think on? Things without all remedy
Should be without regard; what's done is done.
MACBETH We have scorched the snake, not killed it;
She'll close, and be herself, whilst our poor malice
Remains in danger of her former tooth.
But let the frame of things disjoint, both the worlds suffer,
Ere we will eat our meal in fear, and sleep
In the affliction of these terrible dreams
That shake us nightly. Better be with the dead,
Whom we, to gain our peace, have sent to peace, 20
Than on the torture of the mind to lie
In restless ecstasy. Duncan is in his grave;
After life's fitful fever he sleeps well.
Treason has done his worst: nor steel, nor poison,
Malice domestic, foreign levy, nothing
Can touch him further.

27 Gentle my lord *My noble lord*
sleek *smooth*

30 Let . . . Banquo *Remember to give special consideration to Banquo.*
31 Present him eminence *Treat him with special honour*
with eye *showing it in the way you look*
32 Unsafe . . . that *We are unsafe at present so that*
33 lave . . . streams *wash our dignities with streams of flattery – so that they appear to be unsullied*
34 vizards *masks – compare I. 7. 82. In this and the previous image there is again an echo of the theme of clothes.*
35 leave this *stop thinking in this way*
36 full of scorpions *Possibly a reference to the belief that scorpions would breed in one's brain if one smelt the herb basil.*
38 copy *copyhold, a form of lease – nature has not given them an eternal lease of life*
40 jocund *joyful*
41 cloistered *secluded, furtive – perhaps with an allusion to bats' frequenting old churches*
42 shard-borne *borne on scaly wings; or perhaps 'shard-born', born in dung*
43 yawning *that lulls one to sleep – the curfew bell*
44 note *notoriety. The word continues the sense of 'peal'.*

45 Be . . . chuck *This marks a striking change in their relationship. Macbeth's term of endearment, 'chuck', is condescending.*
46 seeling *blinding. A falcon's eyes were 'seeled' when the eyelids were sewn together in order to tame it. Compare I. 4. 50–3 and I. 5. 49–53.*
49 bond *Banquo's lease of life (see l. 38), with perhaps an allusion to the witches' promise to him. 'Seeling' – suggesting 'sealing' – contributes to the legal metaphor.*
50 thickens *See I. 5. 49 and note.*
51 rooky *full of rooks*
53 night's . . . agents *the 'murd'ring ministers' (I. 5. 47)*

LADY MACBETH Come on;
Gentle my lord, sleek o'er your rugged looks,
Be bright and jovial among your guests tonight.
MACBETH So shall I, love, and so I pray be you.
Let your remembrance apply to Banquo, 30
Present him eminence both with eye and tongue–
Unsafe the while, that we
Must lave our honours in these flattering streams,
And make our faces vizards to our hearts,
Disguising what they are.
LADY MACBETH You must leave this.
MACBETH O, full of scorpions is my mind, dear wife!
Thou know'st that Banquo, and his Fleance, lives.
LADY MACBETH But in them nature's copy's not eterne.
MACBETH There's comfort yet; they are assailable.
Then be thou jocund. Ere the bat hath flown 40
His cloistered flight, ere to black Hecate's summons
The shard-borne beetle with his drowsy hums
Hath rung night's yawning peal, there shall be done
A deed of dreadful note.
LADY MACBETH What's to be done?
MACBETH Be innocent of the knowledge, dearest chuck,
Till thou applaud the deed. Come, seeling night,
Scarf up the tender eye of pitiful day,
And with thy bloody and invisible hand
Cancel and tear to pieces that great bond
Which keeps me pale. Light thickens, and the crow 50
Makes wing to the rooky wood.
Good things of day begin to droop and drowse,
Whiles night's black agents to their preys do rouse.
Thou marvell'st at my words; but hold thee still,

55 Things . . . ill *Actions that begin with evil need more crimes to consolidate them.*

ACT THREE, scene 3

[three MURDERERS] *The identity of the third murderer has fascinated critics. Johnson thought that he was 'the perfect spy o' the time' to whom Macbeth referred (III. 1. 129), while others have suggested that he represents 'destiny', or is Macbeth himself – but in that case Macbeth would have known of the escape of Fleance before the next scene. His appearance suggests the nervous uncertainty in which Macbeth lives, unable to trust his own two assassins.*

2 He . . . mistrust *We need not mistrust him*
2–3 delivers . . . offices *tells us our duties*
4 To . . . just *Just as Macbeth directed*
6 lated *belated*
7 timely *welcome at such a time*
8 subject . . . watch *man we are watching for*

10 note . . . expectation *list of expected guests*
11 go about *go the long way round – Banquo was calling the grooms who would lead them.*

15 Stand to't *Stand ready for it.*
16 Let . . . down *i.e. it won't matter to you*

Things bad begun make strong themselves by ill.
So, prithee, go with me. [*Exeunt*

Scene 3. *Enter three* MURDERERS

FIRST MURDERER But who did bid thee join with us?
THIRD MURDERER Macbeth.
SECOND MURDERER He needs not our mistrust, since he delivers
Our offices, and what we have to do,
To the direction just.
FIRST MURDERER Then stand with us.
The west yet glimmers with some streaks of day;
Now spurs the lated traveller apace
To gain the timely inn, and near approaches
The subject of our watch.
THIRD MURDERER Hark! I hear horses.
BANQUO [*Within*] Give us a light there, ho!
SECOND MURDERER Then 'tis he. The rest
That are within the note of expectation 10
Already are i' the court.
FIRST MURDERER His horses go about.
THIRD MURDERER Almost a mile; but he does usually,
So all men do, from hence to the palace gate
Make it their walk.

Enter BANQUO *and* FLEANCE, *with a torch*

SECOND MURDERER A light, a light!
THIRD MURDERER 'Tis he.
FIRST MURDERER Stand to't.
BANQUO It will be rain tonight.
FIRST MURDERER Let it come down.

FIRST MURDERER *strikes out the torch, and they attack* BANQUO *and* FLEANCE

BANQUO O treachery! Fly, good Fleance, fly, fly, fly!
Thou mayst revenge – O slave!

BANQUO *falls*; FLEANCE *escapes*

19 Was't . . . way *Wasn't that how we were to do it? It sounds as if there was some lack of understanding between the third murderer and the others – perhaps it is Macbeth's extra precaution that causes the 'botching'.*

21 Best half *the most important part*

ACT THREE, scene 4

This is a ceremonial state banquet representing what should have been Macbeth's triumph as a king, surrounded by his thanes. For Shakespeare and his contemporaries ceremony was not an empty form, but the gracious recognition of that 'order' on which the health of society depends, as the health of the body depends on the nourishment that the banquet provides – 'the sauce to meat is ceremony' (l. 35). There is repeated stress on 'degrees' (l. 1), 'state' (l. 5), and 'duty' (l. 91), contrasted with the physical brutalities of murder (ll. 26, 78–81) and the disorder of usurpation (ll. 109, 118).

1 degrees *ranks, determining the order in which they sit*

1–2 At . . . last *From beginning to end*

3 society *the company*

4 the . . . host *as the genial landlord of a tavern. But he is only acting the part, he will 'play' it.*

5 state *chair of state, covered with a canopy – perhaps set in the inner stage. It is now Lady Macbeth who has to 'keep alone' (compare III. 2. 8), while Macbeth plays the gracious host, rather too self-consciously.*

in best time *at the right time*

6 require . . . welcome *request her to welcome you*

9 encounter *greet*

10 Both . . . even *either, now the hostess and her guests are equal in courtesy, or, both sides of the table are equally full*

11 large *liberal*

11–12 we'll . . . round *I'll drink a toast to the whole company*

18 the nonpareil *without an equal*

THIRD MURDERER Who did strike out the light?
FIRST MURDERER Was't not the way?
THIRD MURDERER There's but one down; the son is fled.
SECOND MURDERER We have lost 20
Best half of our affair.
FIRST MURDERER Well, let's away,
And say how much is done. [*Exeunt*

Scene 4. *A banquet prepared. Enter* MACBETH, LADY MACBETH, ROSS, LENNOX, LORDS, *and* ATTENDANTS

MACBETH You know your own degrees, sit down. At first
And last, the hearty welcome.
LORDS Thanks to your Majesty.
MACBETH Ourself will mingle with society,
And play the humble host.
Our hostess keeps her state, but in best time
We will require her welcome.
LADY MACBETH Pronounce it for me, sir, to all our friends,
For my heart speaks they are welcome.
Enter FIRST MURDERER, *to the door*
MACBETH See, they encounter thee with their hearts' thanks.
Both sides are even; here I'll sit i' the midst. 10
Be large in mirth; anon we'll drink a measure
The table round. [*Goes to the door*
There's blood upon thy face.
MURDERER 'Tis Banquo's then.
MACBETH 'Tis better thee without than he within.
Is he dispatched?
MURDERER My lord, his throat is cut;
That I did for him.
MACBETH Thou art the best o' the cut-throats;
Yet he's good that did the like for Fleance.
If thou didst it, thou art the nonpareil.
MURDERER Most royal sir, – Fleance is 'scaped.

20 fit *spasm of fear and frustration*
perfect *completely secure*
21 whole *sound, solid*
founded *on as firm foundations*
22 broad and general *unconfined, free*
casing *enclosing. The repetition shows his neurotic fixation on the theme.*
23 cabined, cribbed *enclosed as in a cabin or crib ('hovel')*
24 saucy *persistently intruding*
safe *securely dealt with*
26 trenched *deeply cut*
27 a death ... nature *sufficient to kill a normal man*

28 worm *serpent. Compare III. 2. 13.*
29 nature ... breed *qualities that in time will be dangerous*
31 hear ourselves *speak to each other*
32 the cheer *hospitable encouragement. Consider how the thanes and Lady Macbeth would have been behaving while Macbeth talked with the murderer.*
32–4 The feast ... welcome *It is no better than a meal that one has to pay for if the guests are not often assured, while it is in progress, that it is given hospitably*
34 To feed ... home *Mere eating is best done at home*
35 From ... ceremony *When one is away from home it is the courteous entertainment that gives food its special savour.*
36 Meeting ... bare *Social gatherings would be barren. For the benefit of the guests she lightens the rebuke with the pun on 'meat' and 'meeting'.*
remembrancer *one who reminds*
37 wait on *follow*
39 country's ... roofed *all the nobility of our country under one roof, or, the assembly of our nobility completed, as a house is completed by its roof – implying that Banquo is the highest part of the structure.*
40 graced *full of grace – with also a veiled reference to his having been 'sent to grace'*
[The GHOST ... place] *The Folio puts the entrance at l. 36, but when Dr Samuel Forman saw the play at the Globe in 1611 he recorded that it entered when Macbeth mentioned Banquo. The ghost is probably an illusion since only Macbeth sees it; moreover, it appears when he is thinking of Banquo and disappears when he regains his self-control and challenges it (ll. 69–72, 105–6).*

MACBETH Then comes my fit again. I had else been perfect; 20
Whole as the marble, founded as the rock,
As broad and general as the casing air;
But now I am cabined, cribbed, confined, bound in
To saucy doubts and fears. But Banquo's safe?

MURDERER Ay, my good lord; safe in a ditch he bides,
With twenty trenched gashes on his head,
The least a death to nature.

MACBETH Thanks for that.
There the grown serpent lies; the worm that's fled
Hath nature that in time will venom breed,
No teeth for the present. Get thee gone; tomorrow 30
We'll hear ourselves again. [*Exit* MURDERER

LADY MACBETH My royal lord,
You do not give the cheer. The feast is sold
That is not often vouched, while 'tis a-making,
'Tis given with welcome. To feed were best at home;
From thence, the sauce to meat is ceremony;
Meeting were bare without it.

MACBETH Sweet remembrancer!
Now good digestion wait on appetite,
And health on both.

LENNOX May't please your Highness sit.

MACBETH Here had we now our country's honour roofed,
Were the graced person of our Banquo present; 40

The GHOST *of* BANQUO *enters, and sits in* MACBETH'S *place*

Who may I rather challenge for unkindness
Than pity for mischance.

ROSS His absence, sir,
Lays blame upon his promise. Please 't your Highness
To grace us with your royal company?

41–2 Who . . . mischance *Whom I hope I may rebuke for discourtesy, rather than have to pity for some accident that has delayed him*

unkindness *impropriety – conduct that is 'unnatural' when one is invited to dinner*

43 Lays . . . promise *Makes him blameworthy for promising what he could not fulfil*

48 done this *played this trick, or, murdered Banquo*

49 did it *killed you. The feeble equivocation shows how desperate he is.*

54 upon a thought *with the speed of thought*

55 note *take notice of*

56 offend *harm*

extend his passion *prolong his agitation*

57 Feed . . . not *To what extent would they obey this command during the dialogue that follows?*

Are . . . man? *Compare I. 7. 46–51.*

59 proper stuff! *fine nonsense!*

60 very . . . fear *nothing but the fanciful imagining prompted by your fear*

61 air-drawn *drawn in the air*

62 flaws *outbursts – a 'flaw' was a gust of wind*

63 Imposters . . . fear *Not genuine fear, since there is nothing to be feared.*

65 Authorised . . . grandam *Told on the authority of her grandmother – an old wives' tale.*

69 nod *The ghost has been shaking its head accusingly at him – see ll. 49–50.*

70 charnel-houses *store-houses for the bones of the dead*

71 monuments *tombs*

72 maws *stomachs. The dead cannot return after being digested by a kite.*

unmanned in folly? *is your manhood destroyed by this foolishness?*

MACBETH The table's full.

LENNOX Here is a place reserved, sir.

MACBETH Where?

LENNOX Here, my good lord. – What is't that moves your Highness?

MACBETH Which of you have done this?

LORDS What, my good lord?

MACBETH [*To the* GHOST] Thou canst not say I did it; never shake
Thy gory locks at me. 50

ROSS Gentlemen, rise; his Highness is not well.

LADY MACBETH Sit, worthy friends. My lord is often thus,
And hath been from his youth. Pray you, keep seat;
The fit is momentary, upon a thought
He will again be well. If much you note him,
You shall offend him and extend his passion.
Feed, and regard him not. [*To* MACBETH] Are you a man?

MACBETH Ay, and a bold one, that dare look on that
Which might appal the devil.

LADY MACBETH O proper stuff!
This is the very painting of your fear. 60
This is the air-drawn dagger which you said
Led you to Duncan. O, these flaws and starts,
Impostors to true fear, would well become
A woman's story at a winter's fire,
Authorised by her grandam. Shame itself!
Why do you make such faces? When all's done,
You look but on a stool.

MACBETH Prithee, see there!
Behold! look! lo! How say you?
Why, what care I! If thou canst nod, speak too.
If charnel-houses and our graves must send 70
Those that we bury back, our monuments
Shall be the maws of kites. [*Exit* GHOST

LADY MACBETH What, quite unmanned in folly?

75 humane . . . weal *humane (or human) laws purged the commonwealth of barbarism, and civilised it*

77 The . . . been *i.e. always until now, in both barbarous and civilised times*

80 mortal murders *fatal wounds*

81–2 more . . . is *more unnatural even than the murder of Banquo*

83 lack you *miss your company*

84 muse *wonder*

90 To all . . . thirst *I long to drink to all, and to Banquo – Macbeth's return to Banquo seems compulsive*

91 all to all *all good health to all, or, all shall drink to all*

the pledge *i.e. of loyalty*

92 Avaunt *Away*

94 speculation *consciousness*

96 thing of custom *normal occurrence*

MACBETH If I stand here, I saw him.

LADY MACBETH Fie, for shame!

MACBETH Blood hath been shed ere now, i' the olden time,
Ere humane statute purged the gentle weal;
Ay, and since too, murders have been performed
Too terrible for the ear. The time has been
That when the brains were out the man would die,
And there an end. But now they rise again,
With twenty mortal murders on their crowns, 80
And push us from our stools. This is more strange
Than such a murder is.

LADY MACBETH My worthy lord,
Your noble friends do lack you.

MACBETH I do forget.
Do not muse at me, my most worthy friends;
I have a strange infirmity, which is nothing
To those that know me. Come, love and health to all;
Then I'll sit down. Give me some wine; fill full.
I drink to the general joy o' the whole table,
And to our dear friend Banquo, whom we miss;

Enter GHOST

Would he were here! To all, and him, we thirst, 90
And all to all.

LORDS Our duties, and the pledge.

MACBETH [*To the* GHOST] Avaunt, and quit my sight! Let the earth hide thee!
Thy bones are marrowless, thy blood is cold;
Thou hast no speculation in those eyes
Which thou dost glare with!

LADY MACBETH Think of this, good peers,
But as a thing of custom. 'Tis no other;
Only it spoils the pleasure of the time.

MACBETH What man dare, I dare.
Approach thou like the rugged Russian bear,

100 Hyrcan *The tigers of Hircania, the region south of the Caspian, are mentioned in Pliny's* Natural History.

101 nerves *sinews*

103 dare ... desert *challenge me to single combat, where I can expect no assistance*

104 If ... inhabit *If I live in fear, or, if I entertain feelings of fear ('inhabit' could mean 'house')*

protest *proclaim*

105 baby ... girl *girl's doll, or, a mere baby of a girl*

108 displaced *driven away*

109 admired *causing astonishment*

disorder *of his mind and behaviour*

110 overcome *pass over*

like ... cloud *insubstantial, and causing no surprise*

111–12 You ... owe *You make even my own nature seem strange to me. He doubts either the courage that he thought he possessed, or whether he could have been so fearful.*

115 mine *the 'natural ruby' – redness – of his cheeks*

118 Stand ... going *Do not bother about the correct procedure of leave-taking. Compare l. 1.*

119 at once *all together – ignoring precedence*

119–20 better ... Majesty *Is this ironic?*

121 It *i.e. Banquo's murder*

blood ... blood *murder will be revenged by murder. Compare I. 7. 8–12.*

122 Stones ... move *i.e. to disclose the body of a murdered man*

trees to speak *i.e. to expose a murderer – as the ghost of Polydorus speaks from a tree in Virgil's* Aeneid (*iii. 22–68*).

123 Augures *Auguries – the Roman augurs foretold the future from the flight of birds and by examining their entrails.*

understood relations *the understanding of the hidden relationships between auguries and the events they foretell*

124 magot-pies *magpies*

choughs *jackdaws. All three birds mentioned here can be taught to talk, and all of them have sinister associations.*

brought forth *revealed*

125 the night *the time of night. Macbeth shakes off his gloomy meditation and prepares to act.*

The armed rhinoceros, or the Hyrcan tiger, 100
Take any shape but that, and my firm nerves
Shall never tremble. Or be alive again,
And dare me to the desert with thy sword;
If trembling I inhabit then, protest me
The baby of a girl. Hence, horrible shadow!
Unreal mockery, hence! [*Exit* GHOST
Why, so; being gone,
I am a man again. [*To the* LORDS] Pray you, sit still.

LADY MACBETH You have displaced the mirth, broke the good meeting
With most admired disorder.

MACBETH Can such things be,
And overcome us like a summer's cloud, 110
Without our special wonder? You make me strange
Even to the disposition that I owe,
When now I think you can behold such sights
And keep the natural ruby of your cheeks,
When mine is blanched with fear.

ROSS What sights, my lord?

LADY MACBETH I pray you, speak not. He grows worse and worse;
Question enrages him. At once, good night.
Stand not upon the order of your going,
But go at once.

LENNOX Good night; and better health
Attend his Majesty.

LADY MACBETH A kind good night to all. 120

Exeunt all but MACBETH *and* LADY MACBETH

MACBETH It will have blood, they say; blood will have blood.
Stones have been known to move, and trees to speak;
Augures and understood relations have

126 at odds with *disputing with*
which is which *whether it is night or morning*
127 How . . . thou *What do you say to this*
denies his person *refuses to come*
128 Did . . . sir? *She sounds wearily submissive.*
130–1 There's . . . fee'd '*Makbeth had in everie noble mans house one slie fellow or other in fee with him, to reveale all that was said or doone*' (*Holinshed*, Chronicles).
132 betimes *early*
134 worst means *most evil method*
the worst *that can befall*
135 causes *considerations*
135–7 *The image recalls that used by the Captain in praise of Macbeth (I. 2. 39).*
137 go o'er *going on to the other side*
138 Strange . . . hand *I have strange ('unnatural') projects in mind that I will put into practice*
139 scanned *scrutinised – either by others or by Macbeth himself (compare II. 1. 61). The word is linked with 'acted' as an actor was said to 'scan' his part when he studied it.*
140 season *preservative*
142 initiate *that of a novice*
wants hard use *needs to be hardened by practice and familiarity*
143 young in deed *inexperienced in bloody deeds*

ACT THREE, scene 5

This scene, and ll. 39–43 and 125–32 of IV. 1., are generally included in the play, but are almost certainly not by Shakespeare. They are irrelevant to the plot and, while they were probably added because of the popularity of the witch scenes, they actually reduce their impact – Hecate (see II. 1. 52 and note) speaks like an indignant schoolmistress. All three passages have the same tripping iambic metre, in contrast to the grim trochaic verse of Shakespeare's witches, and the two songs and the dance that conclude them are quite out of character – 'Like elves and fairies in a ring' (IV. 1. 42). The songs come from Middleton's The Witch, *but the octosyllabic verse was probably added by some other writer.*

1 how now? *what's the matter?*
angerly *angrily*

By magot-pies and choughs and rooks brought forth
The secret'st man of blood. What is the night?

LADY MACBETH Almost at odds with morning, which is which.

MACBETH How say'st thou, that Macduff denies his person
At our great bidding?

LADY MACBETH Did you send to him, sir?

MACBETH I hear it by the way; but I will send.
There's not a one of them but in his house 130
I keep a servant fee'd. I will tomorrow,
(And betimes I will) to the Weird Sisters.
More shall they speak; for now I am bent to know
By the worst means the worst. For mine own good
All causes shall give way. I am in blood
Stepped in so far that, should I wade no more,
Returning were as tedious as go o'er.
Strange things I have in head that will to hand,
Which must be acted ere they may be scanned.

LADY MACBETH You lack the season of all natures, sleep. 140

MACBETH Come, we'll to sleep. My strange and self-abuse
Is the initiate fear that wants hard use: [*Exeunt*
We are yet but young in deed.

Scene 5. *Thunder. Enter the three* WITCHES, *meeting* HECATE

FIRST WITCH Why, how now, Hecate? You look angerly.

HECATE Have I not reason, beldams as you are,
Saucy and overbold? How did you dare
To trade and traffic with Macbeth
In riddles and affairs of death;
And I, the mistress of your charms,

2 beldams *old hags*
3 Saucy *Presumptuous*
7 close *secret*

11–13 *Most editors agree that the inappropriateness of this to Macbeth is further evidence that the scene is interpolated, but it seems a not inaccurate comment on the conflict within him – he does not love evil itself, but the advantages it can bring him (see I. 4. 50–3).*
15 Acheron *One of the rivers of the Greek underworld*

21 dismal *disastrous*

24 vap'rous drop *It was believed that a magic vapour could be conjured from the moon.*
profound *with mysterious power*
26 sleights *secret devices*
27 artificial sprites *spirits conjured up by magical arts – the apparitions*
29 confusion *destruction*
30–1 bear . . . wisdom *be guided by his hopes rather than his prudence*

32 security *over-confidence, false security. Again, the interpolator defines the function of the apparitions accurately – he may have been a better critic than a poet.*

34 little spirit *i.e her familiar. In* The Witch *the familiar was lowered in a stage machine designed to look like a cloud, which re-ascended carrying Hecate.*

The close contriver of all harms,
Was never called to bear my part,
Or show the glory of our art?
And, which is worse, all you have done 10
Hath been but for a wayward son,
Spiteful and wrathful, who, as others do,
Loves for his own ends, not for you.
But make amends now; get you gone,
And at the pit of Acheron
Meet me i' the morning. Thither he
Will come to know his destiny.
Your vessels and your spells provide,
Your charms, and every thing beside.
I am for th' air; this night I'll spend 20
Unto a dismal and a fatal end.
Great business must be wrought ere noon:
Upon the corner of the moon
There hangs a vap'rous drop profound;
I'll catch it ere it come to ground;
And that, distilled by magic sleights,
Shall raise such artificial sprites
As, by the strength of their illusion,
Shall draw him on to his confusion.
He shall spurn fate, scorn death, and bear 30
His hopes 'bove wisdom, grace, and fear;
And you all know security
Is mortals' chiefest enemy.
[*Music and a song within*, 'Come away, come away,' etc.]
Hark! I am call'd; my little spirit, see,
Sits in a foggy cloud, and stays for me. [*Exit*

FIRST WITCH Come, let's make haste; she'll soon be back again [*Exeunt*

ACT THREE, scene 6

Another choric scene (see pp 13–14). It is probable that it originally followed IV. 1., and was moved to separate the two witch scenes when III. 5. was added. Macbeth did not decide to send to Macduff until the end of III. iv., at the same time that he said he would visit the witches 'tomorrow,/And betimes', so the Lord could not have heard of Macduff's reception of the messenger before Macbeth visited the witches, and it is unlikely that he would know of Macduff's flight before it was reported by Macbeth's spies (IV. 1. 141–2). The account of Macbeth's exasperation (see ll. 37–9 and note) must also follow this. The time-scale is very condensed, and there are several problems about the character of Lennox (see pp 15–16), but the sequence of events would be more probable if this scene and the next were interchanged.

1 hit *hinted to, or, chimed in with*
2 interpret further *draw their own conclusions*
3 strangely borne *carried out in an odd manner*
4 marry *a mild oath, implying 'but of course'*
7 Men . . . late *The same cynical reason for a man's death is given by the murderer in Kyd's* Spanish Tragedy.
8 cannot . . . thought *can fail to think – 'cannot' with 'want' is a kind of double negative, but, as William Empson pointed out, this is appropriate as Lennox's irony really implies the reverse of what he purports to say.*
13 thralls *captives*
17 borne . . . well *responded admirably to everything – in addition to the general irony, Lennox implies 'to his own advantage'*
19 an't *if it*
21 broad *unrestrained*
24 bestows himself *is staying*
25 holds . . . birth *witholds the hereditary succession to the crown*
27 Of *By*
most . . . Edward *Edward the Confessor*
28–9 the malevolence . . . respect *his misfortunes in no way diminish the respect he is shown*
30 upon his aid *in his support*

Scene 6. *Enter* LENNOX *and another* LORD

LENNOX My former speeches have but hit your thoughts,
Which can interpret further; only I say
Things have been strangely borne. The gracious
Duncan
Was pitied of Macbeth – marry, he was dead;
And the right-valiant Banquo walked too late –
Whom you may say, if't please you, Fleance
killed,
For Fleance fled. Men must not walk too late.
Who cannot want the thought how monstrous
It was for Malcolm and for Donalbain
To kill their gracious father? Damned fact! 10
How it did grieve Macbeth! Did he not straight
In pious rage the two delinquents tear,
That were the slaves of drink and thralls of sleep?
Was not that nobly done? Ay, and wisely too;
For 'twould have angered any heart alive
To hear the men deny't. So that, I say,
He has borne all things well; and I do think
That had he Duncan's sons under his key
(As, an't please heaven, he shall not) they should
find
What 'twere to kill a father; so should Fleance. 20
But peace – for from broad words, and 'cause he
failed
His presence at the tyrant's feast, I hear
Macduff lives in disgrace. Sir, can you tell
Where he bestows himself?

LORD The son of Duncan,
From whom this tyrant holds the due of birth,
Lives in the English Court, and is received
Of the most pious Edward with such grace
That the malevolence of fortune nothing
Takes from his high respect. Thither Macduff
Is gone to pray the holy King, upon his aid 30

31 wake *arouse*

Northumberland . . . Siward *Siward, Earl of Northumberland, and his son, later called 'Young Siward'*

32–3 with . . . work *with God to sanction the enterprise. As Macbeth was an anointed king, rebellion even against his tyranny needed special justification. This scene begins the contrast between the sanctity of Malcom's cause (see also ll. 27, 45–9) and the tyranny of Macbeth, which is summarised in the lines that follow by means of some of the most familiar symbols in the play.*

36 free *not bought by servility or encumbered with guilt*

37–8 this . . . King *Lennox's next words show that the King must be Macbeth, and the report that of Macduff's flight.*

40 with *having been given*

'Sir . . . I' *Macduff's reply*

41 cloudy *sullen*

turns me *turns – 'me' is the ethic dative, which only adds emphasis*

42 hums . . . say *mutters, as if he were saying*

43 clogs *impedes, burdens – the bad news he has to carry would not recommend him to Macbeth (compare V. 5. 33–40)*

44 Advise . . . caution *Warn him to be cautious*

44–5 hold . . . provide *keep as great a distance between himself and Macbeth as, in his wisdom, he can contrive*

48–9 our . . . Under *our country suffering under*

To wake Northumberland and warlike Siward,
That by the help of these, with Him above
To ratify the work, we may again
Give to our tables meat, sleep to our nights,
Free from our feasts and banquets bloody knives,
Do faithful homage, and receive free honours –
All which we pine for now. And this report
Hath so exasperate the King that he
Prepares for some attempt of war.

LENNOX Sent he to Macduff?

LORD He did; and with an absolute 'Sir, not I' 40
The cloudy messenger turns me his back,
And hums, as who should say, 'You'll rue the time
That clogs me with this answer'.

LENNOX And that well might
Advise him to a caution, to hold what distance
His wisdom can provide. Some holy angel
Fly to the court of England and unfold
His message ere he come, that a swift blessing
May soon return to this our suffering country
Under a hand accursed.

LORD I'll send my prayers with him.
[*Exeunt*

ACT FOUR, scene 1

1 Thrice *See I. 3. 10 and note – the magic number recurs in various forms (ll. 61, 65, 77–8, 107–9).*

brinded *streaked, tabby. See I. 1. 8–9 and notes.*

2 hedge-pig *hedgehog*

3 Harpier *the third witch's familiar; H. N. Paul suggests it may be in the form of an owl. The name could be a corruption of 'harpy' – the harpies of Greek mythology were birds with the heads of women.*

5 poisoned entrails *The charm is concocted out of fragments of animals torn from their natural organic life, and almost all the creatures mentioned were thought to be either dangerous or ominous – toads, newts, slow-worms and lizards were supposed to be poisonous.*

8 Sweltered *Sweated. See p 5.*

got *produced*

10 Double . . . trouble *An incantation, suggesting that toil and trouble will be doubled.*

12 Fillet *Slice*

fenny *from the fens*

16 fork *forked tongue*

blind-worm *slow-worm*

17 howlet *owlet*

23 Witches' mummy *a body mummified by witches (see p. 7) – powdered mummy was thought to be medicinal.*

maw and gulf *stomach and gullet*

24 ravined *ravening, or gorged*

25 digged . . . dark *i.e. when its poison would be most deadly*

27 yew *Also considered poisonous, and associated with death because yew trees often grow in graveyards.*

28 Slivered *Sliced off*

the moon's eclipse *an ominous astrological portent*

29 Turk . . . Tartar *Notorious for their savagery and, like the 'blaspheming Jew', for their hostility to Christianity.*

30 birth-strangled *And so unbaptised – see p 6.*

31 Ditch-delivered *Born in a ditch*

drab *whore*

32 slab *coagulated – see p 6.*

ACT FOUR

Scene I. *Thunder. Enter the three* WITCHES

FIRST WITCH Thrice the brinded cat hath mewed.
SECOND WITCH Thrice and once the hedge-pig whined.
THIRD WITCH Harpier cries – 'Tis time, 'tis time.
FIRST WITCH Round about the cauldron go;
In the poisoned entrails throw.
Toad, that under cold stone
Days and nights hast thirty-one
Sweltered venom sleeping got,
Boil thou first i' th' charméd pot.
ALL Double, double, toil and trouble; 10
Fire burn, and cauldron bubble.
SECOND WITCH Fillet of a fenny snake,
In the cauldron boil and bake;
Eye of newt, and toe of frog,
Wool of bat, and tongue of dog,
Adder's fork, and blind-worm's sting,
Lizard's leg, and howlet's wing,
For a charm of powerful trouble,
Like a hell-broth boil and bubble.
ALL Double, double, toil and trouble; 20
Fire burn, and cauldron bubble.
THIRD WITCH Scale of dragon, tooth of wolf,
Witches' mummy, maw and gulf
Of the ravined salt-sea shark,
Root of hemlock digged i' the dark,
Liver of blaspheming Jew,
Gall of goat, and slips of yew
Slivered in the moon's eclipse,
Nose of Turk, and Tartar's lips,
Finger of birth-strangled babe 30
Ditch-delivered by a drab,
Make the gruel thick and slab;

33 chaudron *entrails*
34 ingredience *mixture*

39–43 *See introductory note to III. 5.*
39 commend . . . pains *applaud the trouble you have taken*

46 Open, locks *This might suggest that the setting is some hovel, with a door, but it may be only a conventional formula to admit someone into the magic circle.*

50 conjure . . . profess *call upon you by the black arts that you practise – 'conjuring' was the process by which spirits were summoned and controlled. Macbeth speaks as if he shares their evil power, and his speech has the repetitive form of an incantation.*
51 Howe'er . . . it *i.e. even if it is by communication with the devil. Compare III. 4. 133–4.*
53 yesty *yeasty, foaming*
54 Confound *completely destroy*
navigation *shipping*
55 bladed *unripe – with the ear still in the blade*
lodged *flattened*
57 slope *bend*
59 nature's germens *the seeds of all created things*
tumble all together *The cosmos is reduced to the chaos out of which it was originally created.*
60 sicken *i.e. with the surfeit of disorder*

Add thereto a tiger's chaudron,
For th' ingredience of our cauldron.
ALL Double, double, toil and trouble;
Fire burn, and cauldron bubble.
SECOND WITCH Cool it with a baboon's blood,
Then the charm is firm and good.
Enter HECATE *and the other three* WITCHES
HECATE O, well done! I commend your pains,
And every one shall share i' th' gains. 40
And now about the cauldron sing,
Like elves and fairies in a ring,
Enchanting all that you put in.
Music and a song, 'Black spirits,' *etc.*
[*Exeunt* HECATE *and the other three* WITCHES
SECOND WITCH By the pricking of my thumbs,
Something wicked this way comes:
Open, locks,
Whoever knocks.
Enter MACBETH
MACBETH How now, you secret, black, and midnight hags!
What is't you do?
ALL A deed without a name.
MACBETH I conjure you by that which you profess – 50
Howe'er you come to know it – answer me.
Though you untie the winds and let them fight
Against the churches; though the yesty waves
Confound and swallow navigation up;
Though bladed corn be lodged, and trees blown down;
Though castles topple on their warders' heads;
Though palaces and pyramids do slope
Their heads to their foundations; though the treasure
Of nature's germens tumble all together,
Even till destruction sicken – answer me 60
To what I ask you.

63 our masters *the evil spirits whom they serve*

65 farrow *litter of pigs*
sweaten *sweated*

67 high or low *i.e. in the order of evil spirits*

68 office *function, task*
[Armed Head] *It might appear to Macbeth to be Mac-duff's head, but it is more likely to represent his own (see V. 9. 19). It rises from the cauldron, which might be placed over the trap.*

69 He . . . thought *H. J. C. Grierson pointed out the irony of this, if the head is that of Macbeth.*

74 harped *guessed*

76 [Bloody Child] *representing Macduff (see V. 8. 15–16).*

78 three ears *i.e. one for each repetition of his name. There is a degree of hysteria in his flippancy.*

FIRST WITCH Speak.

SECOND WITCH Demand.

THIRD WITCH We'll answer.

FIRST WITCH Say if thou'dst rather hear it from our mouths,
Or from our masters?

MACBETH Call 'em, let me see 'em.

FIRST WITCH Pour in sow's blood, that hath eaten
Her nine farrow; grease that's sweaten
From the murderer's gibbet, throw
Into the flame.

ALL Come high or low;
Thyself and office deftly show.

Thunder. FIRST APPARITION, *an Armed Head*

MACBETH Tell me, thou unknown power –

FIRST WITCH He knows thy thought;
Hear his speech, but say thou nought. 70

FIRST APPARITION Macbeth, Macbeth, Macbeth! beware Macduff;
Beware the Thane of Fife. Dismiss me. Enough.
[*Descends*

MACBETH Whate'er thou art, for thy good caution thanks;
Thou hast harped my fear aright. But one word more –

FIRST WITCH He will not be commanded. Here's another,
More potent than the first.

Thunder. SECOND APPARITION, *a Bloody Child*

SECOND APPARITION Macbeth, Macbeth, Macbeth!

MACBETH Had I three ears, I'd hear thee.

SECOND APPARITION Be bloody, bold, and resolute; laugh to scorn
The power of man, for none of woman born 80
Shall harm Macbeth. [*Descends*

MACBETH Then live, Macduff; what need I fear of thee?
But yet I'll make assurance double sure,

84 a bond of fate *a legal bond or guarantee, from fate – by killing Macduff he will ensure that fate keeps to the promise that he has just been given.*

85 That . . . lies *So that I am certain that my fears are groundless*

86 thunder *i.e. thunder that reminds him of the evil forces that have seduced him, and of divine wrath.*

[Child . . . Hand] *representing Malcolm and Birnam Wood – the child and the tree unite the symbols of youth and natural fertility. The tree may also represent the family tree of the Stuart kings – see pp 7–8.*

87 issue *offspring*

88–9 round . . . top *the crown*

90 lion-mettled *lion-hearted*

91 chafes *is angry*

frets *complains*

93 Birnam wood *A wooded hill near Dunkeld, twelve miles from Dunsinane.*

95 impress *conscript for military service*

96 bodements *prophecies*

97 Rebellious dead *i.e. Banquo and his future victims – it is useless for them to return (as Banquo did) seeking vengeance. Theobald's emendation to 'Rebellion's head' is often preferred.*

98 our . . . Macbeth *The use of the third person, and the rhymed verse, suggests that he is continuing the prophecy. This speech is sometimes given to one of the witches.*

99 lease of nature *natural length of life – see III. 2. 38*

99–100 pay . . . custom *give up his life (like a debt that has to be repaid to nature) to old age and the normal causes of death*

103 this kingdom *The witches did not specify in which kingdom they would reign.*

106 noise *The term used for a group of musicians.*

And take a bond of fate. Thou shalt not live,
That I may tell pale-hearted fear it lies,
And sleep in spite of thunder.

Thunder. THIRD APPARITION, *a Child Crowned, with a Tree in his Hand*

What is this,
That rises like the issue of a king,
And wears upon his baby brow the round
And top of sovereignty?

ALL Listen, but speak not to't.

THIRD APPARITION Be lion-mettled, proud, and take no care 90
Who chafes, who frets, or where conspirers are.
Macbeth shall never vanquished be until
Great Birnam wood to high Dunsinane hill
Shall come against him. [*Descends*

MACBETH That will never be:
Who can impress the forest, bid the tree
Unfix his earth-bound root? Sweet bodements, good!
Rebellious dead, rise never till the wood
Of Birnam rise; and our high-placed Macbeth
Shall live the lease of nature, pay his breath
To time and mortal custom. Yet my heart 100
Throbs to know one thing: tell me, if your art
Can tell so much, shall Banquo's issue ever
Reign in this kingdom?

ALL Seek to know no more.

MACBETH I will be satisfied. Deny me this,
And an eternal curse fall on you! Let me know. –
Why sinks that cauldron, and what noise is this?
[*Hautboys*

FIRST WITCH Show!

SECOND WITCH Show!

THIRD WITCH Show!

ALL Show his eyes, and grieve his heart; 110
Come like shadows, so depart.

111 [show] *dumb-show*
[eight KINGS] *representing the eight Stuart kings. If Mary Queen of Scots were omitted, the eighth – with the glass – would be James I himself.*

113 hair *The emendation 'air' has been suggested, but 'hair' could mean 'outward appearance'.*

116 Start *i.e. from your sockets*

117 crack of doom *thunder-clap announcing Judgement Day*

119 glass *magical 'perspective glass', showing the future*

121 twofold . . . sceptres *representing the union of the crowns of England and Scotland under James; there are three sceptres as two were used in the English coronation rites.*

123 blood-boltered *with hair matted with blood*

125–32 *See introductory note to III. 5.*

126 amazedly *stupefied*

130 antic round *fantastic round dance*

131–2 That . . . pay *If these lines were interpolated for a royal performance this couplet was probably addressed to the King, as well as to Macbeth.*

132 Our . . . pay *Our homage has given him the welcome that is due to him.*

134 aye *ever*

136 Saw . . . Sisters? *It is very improbable that he would mention the witches to Lennox, but see pp 15–16.*

138 Infected . . . ride *See p 6. It was thought that plague was carried by the air.*

139 damned . . . them *He damns himself.*

A show of eight KINGS, *the last with a Glass in his hand; the* GHOST *of* BANQUO *following*

MACBETH Thou art too like the spirit of Banquo; down!
Thy crown does sear mine eyeballs. And thy hair,
Thou other gold-bound brow, is like the first. –
A third is like the former. Filthy hags!
Why do you show me this? A fourth? Start, eyes!
What, will the line stretch out to the crack of doom?
Another yet? A seventh? I'll see no more;
And yet the eighth appears, who bears a glass
Which shows me many more; and some I see 120
That twofold balls and treble sceptres carry.
Horrible sight! Now I see 'tis true,
For the blood-boltered Banquo smiles upon me,
And points at them for his. What! is this so?

FIRST WITCH Ay, sir, all this is so. But why
Stands Macbeth thus amazedly?
Come, sisters, cheer we up his sprites,
And show the best of our delights.
I'll charm the air to give a sound,
While you perform your antic round, 130
That this great king may kindly say
Our duties did his welcome pay.

Music. The WITCHES *dance, and vanish*

MACBETH Where are they? Gone? Let this pernicious hour
Stand aye accursèd in the calendar!
Come in, without there!

Enter LENNOX

LENNOX What's your Grace's will?

MACBETH Saw you the Weird Sisters?

LENNOX No, my lord.

MACBETH Came they not by you?

LENNOX No, indeed, my lord.

MACBETH Infected be the air whereon they ride,
And damned all those that trust them. I did hear

ACT IV, SCENE 2

144 anticipat'st *forestalls*

145–6 The flighty . . . it *Your actions will never catch up with your intentions unless you act immediately – the act accompanies the thought.*
flighty *speedy*

147–8 The very . . . hand *I shall act at once, on my first impulse.*
firstlings *firstborn*

149 crown *complete*

153 trace . . . line *follow him in line of descent*

154 This . . . cool *Compare II. 1. 61.*

155 sights *the apparitions*

ACT FOUR, scene 2

This scene is used to epitomise the general terror throughout Scotland. The destructive forces of disorder – vividly described by Ross as a shifting chaos in which all the foundations of certainty are sapped away – are contrasted with the natural order of family relationships, and of birth and growth (see ll. 9–11, 32–6, 85–6).

3–4 when . . . traitors *even when we have not acted treacherously our fear makes us appear treacherous, by causing us to flee*

The galloping of horses. Who was't came by? 140

LENNOX 'Tis two or three, my lord, that bring you word
Macduff is fled to England.

MACBETH Fled to England?

LENNOX Ay, my good lord.

MACBETH [*Aside*] Time, thou anticipat'st my dread exploits:
The flighty purpose never is o'ertook
Unless the deed go with it. From this moment
The very firstlings of my heart shall be
The firstlings of my hand. And even now,
To crown my thoughts with acts, be it thought and done:
The castle of Macduff I will surprise, 150
Seize upon Fife, give to th' edge o' the sword
His wife, his babes, and all unfortunate souls
That trace him in his line. No boasting like a fool;
This deed I'll do before this purpose cool.
But no more sights! [*Aloud*] Where are these gentlemen?
Come, bring me where they are. [*Exeunt*

Scene 2. *Enter* LADY MACDUFF, *her* SON, *and* ROSS

LADY MACDUFF What had he done, to make him fly the land?

ROSS You must have patience, madam.

LADY MACDUFF He had none.
His flight was madness; when our actions do not,
Our fears do make us traitors.

ROSS You know not
Whether it was his wisdom or his fear.

LADY MACDUFF Wisdom! To leave his wife, to leave his babes,

7 titles *possessions – what he is entitled to*

9 wants *lacks*
touch *instinct*

11 owl *The owl is mentioned ominously before each of the three murders in the play.*

12 All . . . love *He is motivated only by fear for himself, not at all by love for us.*

14 coz *Used for any degree of relationship – see note to I. 2. 24.*

15 school *discipline, control*
for *as for*

17 fits . . . season *convulsions of the times. Compare III. 4. 20 – Macbeth's disease has infected his kingdom.*

18 are traitors *are declared to be traitors*

19 know ourselves *know that we are traitors*

19–20 hold . . . fear *our fear makes us believe rumours*

22 Each . . . move *In contrary directions and move aimlessly*

23 Shall *it will*
but *before*

24 Things . . . upward *When things are at the worst they must either end altogether or else improve.*

29 my disgrace *i.e. because he would weep*
discomfort *embarrassment*

30 Sirrah *Used affectionately*

32 As birds do *See* Matthew, *vi. 26.*
with *on*

33 get *can find*

34 lime *bird lime, used to catch birds*

35 pitfall *snare*
gin *trap*

His mansion, and his titles in a place
From whence himself does fly? He loves us not:
He wants the natural touch; for the poor wren,
The most diminutive of birds, will fight, 10
Her young ones in her nest, against the owl.
All is the fear, and nothing is the love;
As little is the wisdom, where the flight
So runs against all reason.

ROSS My dearest coz,
I pray you school yourself. But, for your husband,
He is noble, wise, judicious, and best knows
The fits o' th' season. I dare not speak much further;
But cruel are the times, when we are traitors
And do not know ourselves; when we hold rumour
From what we fear, yet know not what we fear, 20
But float upon a wild and violent sea
Each way, and move. I take my leave of you.
Shall not be long but I'll be here again.
Things at the worst will cease, or else climb upward
To what they were before. My pretty cousin,
Blessing upon you!

LADY MACDUFF Fathered he is, and yet he's fatherless.

ROSS I am so much a fool, should I stay longer,
It would be my disgrace and your discomfort.
I take my leave at once. [*Exit*

LADY MACDUFF Sirrah, your father's dead, 30
And what will you do now? How will you live?

SON As birds do, mother.

LADY MACDUFF What, with worms and flies?

SON With what I get, I mean; and so do they.

LADY MACDUFF Poor bird, thou'dst never fear the net nor lime,
The pitfall nor the gin.

36 Poor . . . for *No one bothers to trap* poor *birds.*

38 do for *find a substitute for*

41 you'll . . . again *if she can come by them so easily she won't value them*

42 wit *intelligence – implying that he hasn't very much and so has to use it all*

43 for thee *for your age*

45 that he was *to his family – but she probably still speaks in a bantering tone*

47–50 *Probably another reference to Garnet – see II. 3. 8–12.*

56 enow *enough*

58 monkey *Used affectionately, perhaps with reference to his cleverness.*

65 in . . . perfect *I am well acquainted with your rank – I know who you are.*

66 doubt *fear*
nearly *closely*

67 homely *humble*

SON Why should I, mother?
Poor birds they are not set for.
My father is not dead, for all your saying.

LADY MACDUFF Yes, he is dead. How wilt thou do for a father?

SON Nay, how will you do for a husband?

LADY MACDUFF Why, I can buy me twenty at any market. 40

SON Then you'll buy 'em to sell again.

LADY MACDUFF Thou speak'st with all thy wit, and yet i' faith
With wit enough for thee.

SON Was my father a traitor, mother?

LADY MACDUFF Ay, that he was.

SON What is a traitor?

LADY MACDUFF Why, one that swears and lies.

SON And be all traitors that do so?

LADY MACDUFF Every one that does so is a traitor, and must be hanged. 50

SON And must they all be hanged that swear and lie?

LADY MACDUFF Every one.

SON Who must hang them?

LADY MACDUFF Why, the honest men.

SON Then the liars and swearers are fools; for there are liars and swearers enow to beat the honest men, and hang up them.

LADY MACDUFF Now God help thee, poor monkey. But how wilt thou do for a father?

SON If he were dead, you'd weep for him; if you would 60 not, it were a good sign that I should quickly have a new father.

LADY MACDUFF Poor prattler, how thou talk'st!

Enter a MESSENGER

MESSENGER Bless you, fair dame! I am not to you known,
Though in your state of honour I am perfect.
I doubt some danger does approach you nearly.
If you will take a homely man's advice,

68 little ones *another reference to* Matthew, *xviii.* (*v.* 6
– see note to II. 2. 59.
69 savage *cruel*
70 To do . . . you *either, not to warn her, or, to murder he*
(as others intend)
fell *ruthless*
71 too . . . person *which is already too nearly upon you*

74 earthly *imperfect – in contrast to the celestial world*

82 shag-haired *with shaggy hair*
egg *embryo*
83 fry *spawn – literally, young fish*
84 [Exit LADY MACDUFF] *She is killed off-stage so that her body does not need to be removed from the open stage; her son would be sufficiently small for one of the murderers to carry his body off.*

ACT FOUR, scene 3

This scene is necessary to build up the dramatic stature of Malcolm so that he is a worthy opponent of Macbeth; it contrasts his 'king-becoming graces' with the vices of tyranny, and demonstrates the spiritual power given to a legitimate king (ll. 140–59, 238–9).

3 mortal *deadly*
good *brave*
4 Bestride *Defend – as one stands astride the body of a fallen comrade in battle*
birthdom *country of our birth*

Be not found here; hence, with your little ones.
To fright you thus, methinks I am too savage;
To do worse to you were fell cruelty, 70
Which is too nigh your person. Heaven preserve you!
I dare abide no longer. [*Exit*

LADY MACDUFF Whither should I fly?
I have done no harm. But I remember now
I am in this earthly world, where to do harm
Is often laudable, to do good sometime
Accounted dangerous folly. Why then, alas,
Do I put up that womanly defence
To say I have done no harm?

Enter MURDERERS

What are these faces?

FIRST MURDERER Where is your husband?

LADY MACDUFF I hope in no place so unsanctified 80
Where such as thou mayst find him.

FIRST MURDERER He's a traitor.

SON Thou liest, thou shag-haired villain.

FIRST MURDERER What, you egg! [*Stabs him*
Young fry of treachery!

SON He has killed me, mother;
Run away, I pray you. [*Dies*

Exit LADY MACDUFF, *crying* 'Murder!' *and pursued by the* MURDERERS

Scene 3. *Enter* MALCOLM *and* MACDUFF

MALCOLM Let us seek out some desolate shade, and there
Weep our sad bosoms empty.

MACDUFF Let us rather
Hold fast the mortal sword, and like good men
Bestride our down-fall'n birthdom. Each new morn

5–8 New . . . dolour *Compare I. 7. 18–25.*

6 Strike . . . face *Rebounds from heaven and reverberates through the sky. The metaphor also suggests that Macbeth's crimes have offended heaven.*
that *so that*

8 Like . . . dolour *Similar cries of grief*

8–9 What . . . believe *I will lament what I believe, and believe only what I know to be true.*

10 As *When*
to friend *favourable*

11 perchance *perhaps*

12 whose . . . name *the very mention of whose name*

13 honest *honourable – implying that Macduff may also be only counterfeiting honesty*

14 touched *harmed*

14–15 I . . . me *Although I am only young, you may merit some reward by betraying me.*

15 wisdom *it would be only politic*

16 lamb *himself*

19 recoil *run back from virtue*

20 imperial charge *royal command – continuing the metaphor of a gun recoiling after being fired*

21 That . . . transpose *My thoughts cannot change your nature.*

22 the brightest *Lucifer, Satan's name before his fall – although his brightness was deceptive, true angels are still bright.*

23–4 Though . . . so *Even though everything evil should counterfeit virtue, virtue must still look virtuous – i.e. because Macbeth appeared virtuous before his fall, it does not follow that the appearance of virtue is always deceptive.*

25 where . . . doubts *In Macduff's flight to England – he hoped it would contribute to the overthrow of Macbeth, but its rashness only arouses Malcolm's suspicion of him.*

26 rawness *leaving them exposed to danger*

27 motives *i.e. arousing love*
knots of love *ties of affection*

29–30 Let . . . safeties *Do not regard my suspicions as dishonouring you, but as a protection for me.*

New widows howl, new orphans cry, new sorrows
Strike heaven on the face, that it resounds
As if it felt with Scotland and yelled out
Like syllable of dolour.

MALCOLM What I believe, I'll wail;
What know, believe; and what I can redress,
As I shall find the time to friend, I will. 10
What you have spoke, it may be so perchance.
This tyrant, whose sole name blisters our tongues,
Was once thought honest; you have loved him well;
He hath not touched you yet. I am young, but something
You may deserve of him through me, and wisdom
To offer up a weak, poor, innocent lamb
T' appease an angry god.

MACDUFF I am not treacherous.

MALCOLM But Macbeth is.
A good and virtuous nature may recoil
In an imperial charge. But I shall crave your pardon: 20
That which you are, my thoughts cannot transpose;
Angels are bright still, though the brightest fell;
Though all things foul would wear the brows of grace,
Yet grace must still look so.

MACDUFF I have lost my hopes.

MALCOLM Perchance even there where I did find my doubts.
Why in that rawness left you wife and child,
Those precious motives, those strong knots of love,
Without leave-taking? I pray you,
Let not my jealousies be your dishonours,

30 rightly *truly*

32 lay . . . sure *lay your foundations securely*

33 check *curb*

wrongs *ill-gotten gains – 'wear' again suggests the image of clothes*

34 title *right to the crown*

affeered *confirmed – a legal term.*

36 space *realm*

37 to boot *in addition*

38 as . . . you *from absolute certainty that you are to be feared*

41 withal *in addition*

42 in my right *in support of my right to the throne*

43 England *i.e. the King of England*

44 goodly thousands *i.e. of men*

46 wear *carry*

47 have . . . vices *have to suffer from more vices*

48 more . . . ever *in more various ways than ever before*

49 By *Because of*

What *Who*

51 particulars of vice *individual vices*

grafted *implanted*

52 opened *disclosed and come to maturity, as a flower opens*

55 confineless harms *boundless evils*

57 top *surpass*

58 Luxurious *Lustful*

59 Sudden *Impetuous*

smacking *tasting*

But mine own safeties: you may be rightly just, 30
Whatever I shall think.

MACDUFF Bleed, bleed, poor country!
Great tyranny, lay thou thy basis sure,
For goodness dare not check thee; wear thou thy
wrongs,
The title is affeered. Fare thee well, lord;
I would not be the villain that thou think'st
For the whole space that's in the tyrant's grasp,
And the rich East to boot.

MALCOLM Be not offended;
I speak not as in absolute fear of you.
I think our country sinks beneath the yoke;
It weeps, it bleeds, and each new day a gash 40
Is added to her wounds. I think, withal,
There would be hands uplifted in my right;
And here from gracious England have I offer
Of goodly thousands. But, for all this,
When I shall tread upon the tyrant's head
Or wear it on my sword, yet my poor country
Shall have more vices than it had before,
More suffer, and more sundry ways than ever,
By him that shall succeed.

MACDUFF What should he be?

MALCOLM It is myself I mean; in whom I know 50
All the particulars of vice so grafted
That, when they shall be opened, black Macbeth
Will seem as pure as snow, and the poor state
Esteem him as a lamb, being compared
With my confineless harms.

MACDUFF Not in the legions
Of horrid hell can come a devil more damned
In evils to top Macbeth.

MALCOLM I grant him bloody,
Luxurious, avaricious, false, deceitful,
Sudden, malicious, smacking of every sin
That has a name; but there's no bottom, none, 60

61 voluptuousness *lasciviousness*

63 cistern *stagnant tank*

64 All . . . o'erbear *Overpowering all the barriers of chastity; both meanings of 'continent' – 'chaste' and 'confining' – are relevant here.*

66–7 Boundless . . . tyranny *Intemperance tyrannises over human nature, usurping the place of reason. See p 3.*

67–8 been . . . throne *caused the premature ending of many prosperous reigns*

71 Convey *Secretly manage*

72 cold *chaste*
time *age – see I. 5. 62–3.*
hoodwink *blindfold, deceive*

74 vulture *voracious appetite*

75–6 will . . . inclined *will offer themselves to the king, finding him so inclined*

77 ill-composed affection *unbalanced disposition*

78 staunchless *insatiable*

79 cut off *kill*

80 his *this man's*

81 more-having *acquisitions*

82–3 forge Quarrels *trump up grievances*

85 sticks deeper *is more engrained*

86 summer-seeming *transitory, like the heat of summer – in contrast to more deeply-rooted avarice*

87 sword *cause of death*

88 foisons . . . will *abundance to satisfy your desires*

89 Of . . . own *Merely from your own estates*
portable *bearable*

90 With . . . weighed *Balanced against your virtues*

91 king-becoming graces *virtues appropriate to a king*

92 stableness *stability, constancy*

In my voluptuousness: your wives, your
daughters,
Your matrons, and your maids, could not fill up
The cistern of my lust; and my desire
All continent impediments would o'erbear
That did oppose my will. Better Macbeth,
Than such a one to reign.

MACDUFF Boundless intemperance
In nature is a tyranny; it hath been
The untimely emptying of the happy throne,
And fall of many kings. But fear not yet
To take upon you what is yours: you may 70
Convey your pleasures in a spacious plenty,
And yet seem cold – the time you may so
hoodwink.
We have willing dames enough; there cannot be
That vulture in you to devour so many
As will to greatness dedicate themselves,
Finding it so inclined.

MALCOLM With this there grows
In my most ill-composed affection such
A staunchless avarice that, were I King,
I should cut off the nobles for their lands,
Desire his jewels and this other's house; 80
And my more-having would be as a sauce
To make me hunger more, that I should forge
Quarrels unjust against the good and loyal,
Destroying them for wealth.

MACDUFF This avarice
Sticks deeper, grows with more pernicious root
Than summer-seeming lust; and it hath been
The sword of our slain kings. Yet do not fear;
Scotland hath foisons to fill up your will
Of your mere own. All these are portable,
With other graces weighed. 90

MALCOLM But I have none. The king-becoming graces.
As justice, verity, temperance, stableness,

93 Bounty *Generosity*
lowliness *humility*
94 Devotion *Piety*
95 relish *flavour, trace*
96 division *variations – a term in music*
several *particular*
97–100 *This is a sin that Malcolm does not mention in Holinshed's account. Dover Wilson suggests that it was added to please James, who was working for the reunification of Christendom, and H. N. Paul sees an allusion to the rowdy behaviour of the mob when James and Christian of Denmark were greeted in Cheapside by an allegorical figure representing Concord*
98 Pour ... hell *Compare I. 5. 16, 47. 'Concord' ('harmony') continues the metaphor from music.*
99 Uproar *Cause uproar in*
confound *destroy*
104 untitled *without legal right to the throne*
106 truest issue *true heir*
107 interdiction *exclusion*
108 blaspheme ... breed *slanders his parentage*

110 upon ... knees *in prayer*
111 Died ... lived *It was as if she died to this world in her preparations for the next. See 1* Corinthians, *xv. 31.*
112 repeat'st upon *recite against*
113 Hath ... Scotland *He has no hope of returning if the only possible substitute for Macbeth is equally vicious.*
115 Child ... integrity *This could apply either to Macduff or to his emotion, which derives from his integrity.*
116 black scruples *dark suspicions*
118 trains *plots*
119 modest *discreet, cautious*
121 Deal ... me *Direct the dealings between us.*
122 to *under*
123 Unspeak ... detraction *Withdraw the slanders I spoke against myself.*
abjure *renounce*
125 For strangers *As foreign*

Bounty, perseverance, mercy, lowliness,
Devotion, patience, courage, fortitude –
I have no relish of them, but abound
In the division of each several crime,
Acting it many ways. Nay, had I power, I should
Pour the sweet milk of concord into hell,
Uproar the universal peace, confound
All unity on earth.

MACDUFF O Scotland, Scotland! 100

MALCOLM If such a one be fit to govern, speak.
I am as I have spoken.

MACDUFF Fit to govern!
No, not to live. O nation miserable!
With an untitled tyrant bloody-sceptered,
When shalt thou see thy wholesome days again,
Since that the truest issue of thy throne
By his own interdiction stands accursed,
And does blaspheme his breed? Thy royal father
Was a most sainted King; the Queen that bore
thee,
Oftener upon her knees than on her feet, 110
Died every day she lived. Fare thee well,
These evils thou repeat'st upon thyself
Hath banished me from Scotland. O my breast,
Thy hope ends here!

MALCOLM Macduff, this noble passion,
Child of integrity, hath from my soul
Wiped the black scruples, reconciled my thoughts
To thy good truth and honour. Devilish Macbeth
By many of these trains hath sought to win me
Into his power, and modest wisdom plucks me
From over-credulous haste. But God above 120
Deal between thee and me; for even now
I put myself to thy direction, and
Unspeak mine own detraction; here abjure
The taints and blames I laid upon myself,
For strangers to my nature. I am yet

126 Unknown to woman *Chaste*
was forsworn *committed perjury*

129 The devil *i.e. even the devil*

133 here-approach *coming here*

135 at a point *fully prepared*

136–7 the chance . . . quarrel *may the probability that good will triumph be as well founded as the justice of our cause*

142 stay *await*
convinces *defeats*

143 great . . . art *greatest efforts of medical skill*

145 presently amend *immediately recover*

146 the Evil *i.e. scrofula, the 'king's evil' – see p 4.*

148 since . . . here-remain *during my stay here*

149 solicits *appeal to*

150 strangely-visited *unnaturally afflicted*

152 mere *utter*

153 golden stamp *a specially minted coin stamped with the figure of St Michael. The Tudor monarchs made the sign of the cross with it over the afflicted person, but James regarded this as superstitious and merely hung it round the victim's neck.*

154 spoken *said*

155 succeeding royalty *his royal descendents*

Unknown to woman, never was forsworn,
Scarcely have coveted what was mine own,
At no time broke my faith, would not betray
The devil to his fellow, and delight
No less in truth than life – my first false speaking 130
Was this upon myself. What I am truly
Is thine and my poor country's to command;
Whither, indeed, before thy here-approach,
Old Siward, with ten thousand warlike men
Already at a point, was setting forth.
Now we'll together, and the chance of goodness
Be like our warrănted quarrel. Why are you silent?

MACDUFF Such welcome and unwelcome things at once
'Tis hard to reconcile.

Enter a DOCTOR

MALCOLM Well, more anon.
Comes the King forth, I pray you? 140

DOCTOR Ay, sir; there are a crew of wretched souls
That stay his cure. Their malady convinces
The great assay of art; but at his touch,
Such sanctity hath heaven given his hand,
They presently amend.

MACLCOLM I thank, you, doctor.

[*Exit* DOCTOR

MACDUFF What's the disease he means?

MALCOLM 'Tis called the Evil –
A most miraculous work in this good King,
Which often since my here-remain in England
I have seen him do. How he solicits heaven
Himself best knows; but strangely-visited people, 150
All swoln and ulcerous, pitiful to the eye,
The mere despair of surgery, he cures,
Hanging a golden stamp about their necks,
Put on with holy prayers; and 'tis spoken,
To the succeeding royalty he leaves

156 healing benediction *blessing of healing*
virtue *power*

159 speak him *declare him to be*

160 My countryman *Probably recognisable by his dress.*
161 gentle *noble*
cousin *kinsman*
162 betimes *quickly*
163 means *circumstances*

165 afraid . . . itself *Scotland is alienated from itself in the same way that Macbeth was (Compare II. 2. 73.).*
166–7 nothing . . . nothing *no one, unless he is totally ignorant of the situation*
once *ever*

169 not marked *not noticed – they are so common*

170 modern *commonplace – 'familiar today'*
ecstasy *fit of emotion. Again, Scotland suffers from the same afflictions as its monarch (Compare III. 2. 22, 4. 20.)*
171 scarce . . . who *hardly anyone bothers to ask for whom it is tolled*
173 Dying . . . sicken *Murdered before they have time to fall ill in the natural course of events.*
173–4 relation . . . nice *an account that is only too precise*
175 hiss *cause him to be hissed, because so much happens in an hour that his news has become out of date.*
176 teems *gives birth to, in rapid succession*

The healing benediction. With this strange virtue
He hath a heavenly gift of prophecy,
And sundry blessings hang about his throne
That speak him full of grace.

Enter ROSS

MACDUFF See who comes here.
MALCOLM My countryman; but yet I know him not. 160
MACDUFF My ever-gentle cousin, welcome hither.
MALCOLM I know him now. Good God, betimes remove
The means that makes us strangers!
ROSS Sir, amen.
MACDUFF Stands Scotland where it did?
ROSS Alas, poor country,
Almost afraid to know itself. It cannot
Be called our mother, but our grave: where nothing,
But who knows nothing, is once seen to smile;
Where sighs and groans and shrieks that rend the air
Are made, not marked; where violent sorrow seems
A modern ecstasy. The dead man's knell 170
Is there scarce asked for who, and good men's lives
Expire before the flowers in their caps,
Dying or ere they sicken.
MACDUFF O relation
Too nice, and yet too true!
MALCOLM What's the newest grief?
ROSS That of an hour's age doth hiss the speaker;
Each minute teems a new one.
MACDUFF How does my wife?
ROSS Why, well.
MACDUFF And all my children?
ROSS Well too.
MACDUFF The tyrant has not battered at their peace?

179 well at peace *Compare III. 2. 20.*

180 a niggard *so miserly*

181 the tidings *the news of the murder of Macduff's family, but he still cannot bring himself to deliver it.*

182 heavily borne *sadly carried*

183 out *in the field, against Macbeth*

184 Which . . . rather *My belief in which was the more confirmed*

185 For that *Because*

power a-foot *forces on the march*

186 of *for*

188 doff *throw off – another clothing image, which recalls Macduff's premonition (II. 4. 37–8).*

191–2 An older . . . out *None in Christendom has the reputation of being a more experienced or better soldier.*

194 would *should*

195 latch *catch*

196 general cause *public affairs*

fee-grief *private sorrow – the owner of property held in fee-simple had an absolute, exclusive, right to it.*

197 Due to *Belonging to*

honest *honourable*

202 possess *enthrall – bewitch, as an evil spirit 'possessed' a man (see p 23)*

heaviest sound *saddest words*

203 Humh! *a groan*

205 the manner *the way in which they were killed*

206 quarry *heap of dead animals after a hunt*

deer *punning on 'dear'*

207 the death *i.e. from grief*

ROSS No; they were well at peace when I did leave
'em.

MACDUFF Be not a niggard of your speech. How goes't? 180

ROSS When I came hither to transport the tidings,
Which I have heavily borne, there ran a rumour
Of many worthy fellows that were out;
Which was to my belief witnessed the rather
For that I saw the tyrant's power a-foot.
Now is the time of help; your eye in Scotland
Would create soldiers, make our women fight
To doff their dire distresses.

MALCOLM Be't their comfort
We are coming thither. Gracious England hath
Lent us good Siward and ten thousand men – 190
An older and a better soldier none
That Christendom gives out.

ROSS Would I could answer
This comfort with the like. But I have words
That would be howled out in the desert air,
Where hearing should not latch them.

MACDUFF What concern they?
The general cause; or is it a fee-grief
Due to some single breast?

ROSS No mind that's honest
But in it shares some woe, though the main part
Pertains to you alone.

MACDUFF If it be mine,
Keep it not from me; quickly let me have it. 200

ROSS Let not your ears despise my tongue for ever,
Which shall possess them with the heaviest
sound
That ever yet they heard.

MACDUFF Humh! I guess at it.

ROSS Your castle is surprised; your wife and babes
Savagely slaughtered. To relate the manner
Were, on the quarry of these murdered deer,
To add the death of you.

209–10 *The rhyme indicates the proverbial nature of this saying.*
210 Whispers *Whispers to*
o'er-fraught *over-burdened*

212 must be *had to be*

215 deadly grief *mortal sorrow – both their personal sorrow, that might be alleviated by revenge, and the affliction that distresses Scotland.*
216 He . . . children *Probably referring to Malcom – if he had children he could not have offered such inadequate consolation – but perhaps to Macbeth.*
217 kite *a bird of prey – 'swoop' continues the metaphor*
218 dam *mother – normally used of an animal*
219 fell *fierce*
220 Dispute it *Stand up to it. The theme of manhood returns – see III. 1. 90 and note.*
222 cannot . . . remember *can only remember that*
such things *his wife and children, and the domestic joys he owed to them – his grief prevents him from naming them directly.*
225 Naught *worthless – nothing*
226 demerits *faults*

228 whetstone *grindstone*
229 blunt not *do not make it insensible*

232 intermission *interval – before he faces Macbeth*
233 fiend *Lady Macbeth is later described as 'fiend-like' (V. 9. 35). For the suggestions of demonic possession in the play see pp 23–4.*
234–5 if . . . too *a form of oath – if I let him escape may my punishment be that he also escapes damnation*

MALCOLM Merciful heaven!
What, man, ne'er pull your hat upon your brows;
Give sorrow words. The grief that does not speak
Whispers the o'er-fraught heart and bids it break. 210

MACDUFF My children too?

ROSS Wife, children, servants, all
That could be found.

MACDUFF And I must be from thence!
My wife killed too?

ROSS I have said.

MALCOLM Be comforted;
Let's make us medicines of our great revenge
To cure this deadly grief.

MACDUFF He has no children. – All my pretty ones?
Did you say all? – O hell-kite! – All?
What, all my pretty chickens and their dam
At one fell swoop?

MALCOLM Dispute it like a man.

MACDUFF I shall do so; 220
But I must also feel it as a man.
I cannot but remember such things were
That were most precious to me. Did heaven look
on,
And would not take their part? Sinful Macduff,
They were all struck for thee. Naught that I am,
Not for their own demerits, but for mine,
Fell slaughter on their souls. Heaven rest them
now.

MALCOLM Be this the whetstone of your sword. Let grief
Convert to anger; blunt not the heart, enrage it.

MACDUFF O, I could play the woman with mine eyes, 230
And braggart with my tongue. But gentle
heavens,
Cut short all intermission. Front to front
Bring thou this fiend of Scotland and myself;
Within my sword's length set him; if he scape,
Heaven forgive him too!

236 power *army*

237 Our . . . leave *We need only to take our leave.*

238 ripe . . . shaking *ready to be shaken off the tree*
powers *See note to II. 1. 7.*

239 Put . . . instruments *Incite their human agents, or, perhaps, arm themselves.*
cheer *comfort*

240 The night . . . day *A significant reversal of Macbeth's words (I. 3. 147).*

MALCOLM This tune goes manly.
Come, go we to the King. Our power is ready;
Our lack is nothing but our leave. Macbeth
Is ripe for shaking, and the powers above
Put on their instruments. Receive what cheer you
may;
The night is long that never finds the day. 240
[*Exeunt*

ACT FIVE, scene 1

After the last line of the previous act the scene move[s] immediately to the night that envelopes Scotland, and from the general description of the disorder in the kingdom to th[e] disorder in Lady Macbeth's mind.

1 watched *remained awake*

4 into the field *campaigning against the rebels – see IV 3. 182–5*

5 nightgown *dressing-gown*

6 closet *cabinet for private possessions*

fold it *Kenneth Muir suggests that this is to mark the margin.*

9 perturbation in nature *disturbance in her natural constitution*

9–10 at once *at the same time*

10 do . . . watching *act as if she were awake*

11 slumbery agitation *activity while asleep*

12 actual performances *what she actually does*

14–15 after her *in her words*

16 meet *appropriate*

17–18 having . . . speech *She might otherwise be accused of slandering the Queen.*

18 [taper] *candle*

19 her . . . guise *precisely her manner*

20 close *concealed*

22–3 she . . . continually *Compare I. 5. 49–53.*

ACT FIVE

Scene I. *Enter a* DOCTOR OF PHYSIC *and a* WAITING GENTLEWOMAN

DOCTOR I have two nights watched with you, but can perceive no truth in your report. When was it she last walked?

GENTLEWOMAN Since his Majesty went into the field, I have seen her rise from her bed, throw her nightgown upon her, unlock her closet, take forth paper, fold it, write upon't, read it, afterwards seal it, and again return to bed; yet all this while in a most fast sleep.

DOCTOR A great perturbation in nature, to receive at once the benefit of sleep and do the effects of watching. 10
In this slumbery agitation, besides her walking and other actual performances, what, at any time, have you heard her say?

GENTLEWOMAN That, sir, which I will not report after her.

DOCTOR You may to me, and 'tis most meet you should.

GENTLEWOMAN Neither to you nor any one, having no witness to confirm my speech.

Enter LADY MACBETH *with a taper*

Lo you, here she comes. This is her very guise; and, upon my life, fast asleep. Observe her; stand close. 20

DOCTOR How came she by that light?

GENTLEWOMAN Why, it stood by her; she has light by her continually, 'tis her command.

DOCTOR You see her eyes are open.

GENTLEWOMAN Ay, but their sense is shut.

DOCTOR What is it she does now? Look, how she rubs her hands.

GENTLEWOMAN It is an accustomed action with her, to seem thus washing her hands. I have known her continue in this a quarter of an hour. 30

31 spot *i.e. of blood*

33 satisfy my remembrance *confirm my memory*

35–6 One; two *She imagines she hears a clock. This is often assumed to be the bell that she struck to summon Macbeth to kill Dunçan, but that did not tell her the time.*

36 Hell is murky *A. C. Bradley pointed out that the feature of hell that she most fears is its darkness.*

38–9 when . . . account *when we shall have gained too much power to be asked to account for our deeds. Compare I. 7. 77.*

39–40 Yet . . . him? *Compare II. 2. 55–7. There is still a cynical bluntness in her expression of horror.*

41 mark *notice*

42 The Thane . . . wife *The rhyme is plaintive.*

45 starting *Compare III. 4. 62.*

46 Go to *A mild rebuke*

you *This is generally assumed to refer to Lady Macbeth, but it might well refer to the Gentlewoman.*

50–52 all . . . hand *A parallel statement to Macbeth's (II. 2. 60–3), but now she can consider only concealing the blood, not washing it away. Compare II. 2. 67.*

52–4 sorely charged *heavily burdened*

56 dignity *distinction of being a queen*

59 beyond my practice *too difficult for my skill*

64 on's *of his*

LADY MACBETH Yet here's a spot.

DOCTOR Hark! she speaks. I will set down what comes from her, to satisfy my remembrance the more strongly.

LADY MACBETH Out, damned spot! Out, I say! – One; two; why, then 'tis time to do't. – Hell is murky. – Fie, my lord, fie! A soldier, and afeard? What need we fear who knows it, when none can call our power to account? Yet who would have thought the old man to have had so much blood in him? 40

DOCTOR Do you mark that?

LADY MACBETH The Thane of Fife had a wife; where is she now? – What, will these hands ne'er be clean? – No more o' that, my lord, no more o' that; you mar all with this starting.

DOCTOR Go to, go to; you have known what you should not.

GENTLEWOMAN She has spoke what she should not, I am sure of that; Heaven knows what she has known.

LADY MACBETH Here's the smell of the blood still: all 50 the perfumes of Arabia will not sweeten this little hand. Oh, oh, oh!

DOCTOR What a sigh is there! The heart is sorely charged.

GENTLEWOMAN I would not have such a heart in my bosom for the dignity of the whole body.

DOCTOR Well, well, well.

GENTLEWOMAN Pray God it be, sir.

DOCTOR This disease is beyond my practice. Yet I have known those which have walked in their sleep who 60 have died holily in their beds.

LADY MACBETH Wash your hands, put on your night-gown; look not so pale. – I tell you yet again, Banquo's buried; he cannot come out on's grave.

DOCTOR Even so?

LADY MACBETH To bed, to bed; there's knocking at the gate. Come, come, come, come, give me your hand.

68 What's . . . undone *Perhaps the most poignant echo in the play – see p 26. The torment of Lady Macbeth's hell is the recollection of her past deeds.*

72 Foul whisperings *Rumours of evil deeds*

73 infected *diseased with guilt*

74 discharge *express – continuing the medical image*

75 More . . . divine *i.e. to hear her confession, or perhaps to exorcise the evil spirit in her see p 23*

77 annoyance *harming herself*

78 still *continually*

79 mated *stupified*

ACT FIVE, scene 2

The drum and colours change the mood at once from dark meditation to practical activity. This scene and scenes 4 and 6 are brisk and businesslike.

2 uncle *According to Holinshed, Siward was Duncan's father-in-law, not his brother-in-law, but Shakespeare may have changed the relationship because he made Duncan so much older than the historical King.*

3 Revenges *Desire for revenge*

dear causes *strongly felt motives (causes of action) or grievances ('causes' can mean 'law-suits')*

4 bleeding *bloody*

alarm *call to arms*

5 mortified *dead*

6 well *be likely to*

8 file *list*

10 unrough *beardless*

11 Protest . . . manhood *Demonstrate for the first time that they have reached manhood.*

What's done cannot be undone. To bed, to bed, to bed. [*Exit*

DOCTOR Will she go now to bed? 70

GENTLEWOMAN Directly.

DOCTOR Foul whisperings are abroad. Unnatural deeds
Do breed unnatural troubles; infected minds
To their deaf pillows will discharge their secrets.
More needs she the divine than the physician.
God, God forgive us all! Look after her;
Remove from her the means of all annoyance,
And still keep eyes upon her. So, good night.
My mind she has mated, and amazed my sight;
I think, but dare not speak.

GENTLEWOMAN Good night, good doctor. 80
[*Exeunt*

Scene 2. *Enter, with drum and colours,* MENTEITH, CAITHNESS, ANGUS, LENNOX, *and* SOLDIERS

MENTEITH The English power is near, led on by Malcolm,
His uncle Siward, and the good Macduff.
Revenges burn in them; for their dear causes
Would to the bleeding and the grim alarm
Excite the mortified man.

ANGUS Near Birnam wood
Shall we well meet them; that way are they coming.

CAITHNESS Who knows if Donalbain be with his brother?

LENNOX For certain, sir, he is not. I have a file
Of all the gentry; there is Siward's son,
And many unrough youths that even now 10
Protest their first of manhood.

MENTEITH What does the tyrant?

CAITHNESS Great Dunsinane he strongly fortifies.
Some say he's mad; others, that lesser hate him,

15 distempered *diseased, disordered – the next line suggests a disease such as dropsy, which causes the body to swell*
cause *party, or realm. The word could also mean 'disease' – he has lost control both of his own diseased condition and of his kingdom.*
16 belt of rule *This might suggest a medical regimen as well as the rule of the kingdom – combining the recurrent imagery of disease with that of clothing.*
17 sticking . . . hands *Compare II. 2. 60–1.*
18 minutely *every minute*
upbraid . . . faith-breach *reproach him for his own treachery. Compare I. 7. 10–12.*
19 in command *because they are ordered to*
20 Nothing in love *Not at all from affection for him*
20–2 Now . . . thief *Compare I. 3. 144–7, II. 4. 38.*
23 pestered senses *jangled nerves*
to recoil *for giving way, swinging from one extreme to another*
start *Compare III. 4. 62.*
24–5 all . . . there *his whole being condemns itself*
27 medicine *physician. See pp 3–4. In his* Counterblaste to Tobacco *(1604) James I had written, 'it is the King's part (as the proper Phisician of his Politicke-bodie) to purge it of all those diseases, by Medicines meete for the same'.*
weal *state*
28 in . . . purge *in order to purge our country*
29 of us *of our blood – the suggestion of blood-letting continues the medical image*
30 dew *water*
sovereign *kingly – and a 'sovereign' remedy in medicine is an infallible one*

ACT FIVE, scene 3

3 taint *be tainted with*

5 All . . . consequence *outcome of all human affairs*
me *for, or about, me*

Do call it valiant fury; but, for certain,
He cannot buckle his distempered cause
Within the belt of rule.

ANGUS Now does he feel
His secret murders sticking on his hands;
Now minutely revolts upbraid his faith-breach;
Those he commands move only in command,
Nothing in love. Now does he feel his title 20
Hang loose about him, like a giant's robe
Upon a dwarfish thief.

MENTEITH Who then shall blame
His pestered senses to recoil and start,
When all that is within him does condemn
Itself for being there?

CAITHNESS Well, march we on
To give obedience where 'tis truly owed.
Meet we the medicine of the sickly weal,
And with him pour we, in our country's purge,
Each drop of us.

LENNOX Or so much as it needs
To dew the sovereign flower and drown the weeds. 30
Make we our march towards Birnam.

[*Exeunt, marching*

Scene 3. *Enter* MACBETH, DOCTOR, *and* ATTENDANTS

MACBETH Bring me no more reports; let them fly all.
Till Birnam wood remove to Dunsinane,
I cannot taint with fear. What's the boy Malcolm?
Was he not born of woman? The spirits that know
All mortal consequences have pronounced me thus:
'Fear not, Macbeth; no man that's born of woman

8 English epicures *self-indulgent English*

9 sway *control myself*

11 loon *fool. As it was the name of a water-bird it suggests 'goose' in the next line.*

14 over-red thy fear *cover over your pallor with blood*

15 lily-livered *The liver was thought to be the seat of the emotions, including courage.*

patch *clown*

16 Death . . . soul *May you be damned*

linen *white*

17 Are counsellors *Persuade others*

whey *The pale, thin liquid that is left after milk curdles.*

20 push *onslaught*

21 cheer *perhaps punning on 'cheer' ('hearten') – which follows on from 'sick at heart' – and 'chair' ('enthrone') – which was probably pronounced 'cheer', and leads on to 'disseat' ('dethrone', 'depose').*

22 my . . . life *the course of my life*

23 sere *withered state*

27 mouth-honour *lip-service*

breath *mere air*

28 fain deny *wish to withold*

Shall e'er have power upon thee'. Then fly, false thanes,
And mingle with the English epicures.
The mind I sway by and the heart I bear
Shall never sag with doubt nor shake with fear. 10

Enter a SERVANT

The devil damn thee black, thou cream-faced loon!
Where gott'st thou that goose look?

SERVANT There is ten thousand –

MACBETH Geese, villain?

SERVANT Soldiers, sir.

MACBETH Go prick thy face, and over-red thy fear,
Thou lily-livered boy. What soldiers, patch?
Death of thy soul! those linen cheeks of thine
Are counsellors to fear. What soldiers, whey-face?

SERVANT The English force, so please you.

MACBETH Take thy face hence. [*Exit* SERVANT
Seyton! – I am sick at heart
When I behold – Seyton, I say! – This push 20
Will cheer me ever, or disseat me now.
I have lived long enough: my way of life
Is fall'n into the sere, the yellow leaf;
And that which should accompany old age,
As honour, love, obedience, troops of friends,
I must not look to have; but, in their stead,
Curses, not loud but deep, mouth-honour, breath,
Which the poor heart would fain deny, and dare not.
Seyton!

Enter SEYTON

SEYTON What's your gracious pleasure?

MACBETH What news more? 30

SEYTON All is confirmed, my lord, which was reported.

35 moe *more*
skirr *scour*

38 thick-coming *crowding upon each other – compare the use of 'thick' in I. 5. 42. Macbeth has ignored the doctor, who must have been waiting nervously – he has to be very cautious in reporting the symptoms he has observed.*
40 minister to *prescribe for*
41 rooted *deeply implanted*
42 Raze out *erase.*
written troubles of *troubles imprinted on*
43 oblivious *causing forgetfulness*
44 stuffed *clogged with guilt*
perilous stuff *the melancholy 'humour' that was thought to be the cause of grief and madness.*

48 staff *the insignia of a commanding officer*

50 dispatch *hurry*
50–1 cast . . . water *diagnose its disease by examining its urine*

52 pristine *first, and unsullied. Compare V. 2. 27–9.*

54 Pull't off *Pull it off – i.e. some part of his armour which his agitation has prevented Seyton from fixing properly. His behaviour throughout this scene confirms Angus's description (V. 2. 23).*

57–8 your . . . something *A cautious reply to what may have been a suspicious question. The doctor's canniness was evident in, for example, V. 1. 46–7.*
58 it *See l. 54.*
59 bane *destruction*

MACBETH I'll fight, till from my bones my flesh be hacked.
Give me my armour.
SEYTON 'Tis not needed yet.
MACBETH I'll put it on.
Send out moe horses, skirr the country round;
Hang those that talk of fear. Give me mine armour. –
How does your patient, doctor?
DOCTOR Not so sick, my lord,
As she is troubled with thick-coming fancies
That keep her from her rest.
MACBETH Cure her of that:
Canst thou not minister to a mind diseased, 40
Pluck from the memory a rooted sorrow,
Raze out the written troubles of the brain,
And with some sweet oblivious antidote
Cleanse the stuffed bosom of that perilous stuff
Which weighs upon the heart?
DOCTOR Therein the patient
Must minister to himself.
MACBETH Throw physic to the dogs, I'll none of it. –
Come, put mine armour on; give me my staff.
Seyton, send out. – Doctor, the thanes fly from me. –
Come sir, dispatch. If thou couldst, doctor, cast 50
The water of my land, find her disease,
And purge it to a sound and pristine health,
I would applaud thee to the very echo,
That should applaud again. – Pull't off, I say. –
What rhubarb, senna, or what purgative drug
Would scour these English hence? Hear'st thou of them?
DOCTOR Ay, my good lord; your royal preparation
Makes us hear something.
MACBETH Bring it after me. –
I will not be afraid of death and bane

62 Profit . . . here *Doctors were notorious for avarice. The jingling rhyme of this prudent comment echoes that of Macbeth's final couplet, and shows up its empty bravado.*

ACT FIVE, scene 4

2 chambers *bedchambers – when we can sleep in safety. Compare III. 6. 34.*
nothing *not at all*

5 shadow *conceal*
6 discovery *reconaissance*

8 no . . . but *nothing else but that – all reports agree*
9–10 endure . . . it *allow us to lay siege to it*

11 advantage . . . gone *opportunity to escape*
12 more and less *those of high and low rank*
given . . . revolt *rebelled against him*
13 constrained things *wretches who are compelled to*
14–16 Let . . . soldiership *Our accurate assessment (of the situation) must await its actual outcome, so let us confine ourselves to the practical business of fighting – he reproves Malcolm's youthful confidence.*

17 due *at the appropriate time*
18 we have . . . owe *are our advantages and our disadvantages – our credits and debits*
19–20 Thoughts . . . arbitrate *Speculation can only suggest uncertain hopes, but the issue can only be decided by fighting.*
21 advance *proceed with*

Till Birnam forest come to Dunsinane. 60
[*Exeunt all but* DOCTOR

DOCTOR Were I from Dunsinane away and clear,
Profit again should hardly draw me here.
[*Exit*

Scene 4. *Enter, with drum and colours,* MALCOLM, SIWARD, MACDUFF, YOUNG SIWARD, MENTEITH, CAITHNESS, ANGUS, LENNOX, ROSS, *and* SOLDIERS, *marching*

MALCOLM Cousins, I hope the days are near at hand
That chambers will be safe.
MENTEITH We doubt it nothing.
SIWARD What wood is this before us?
MENTEITH The wood of Birnam.
MALCOLM Let every soldier hew him down a bough
And bear't before him; thereby shall we shadow
The numbers of our host, and make discovery
Err in report of us.
SOLDIERS It shall be done.
SIWARD We learn no other but the confident tyrant
Keeps still in Dunsinane, and will endure
Our setting down before 't.
MALCOLM 'Tis his main hope, 10
For where there is advantage to be gone
Both more and less have given him the revolt,
And none serve with him but constrainéd things
Whose hearts are absent too.
MACDUFF Let our just censures
Attend the true event, and put we on
Industrious soldiership.
SIWARD The time approaches
That will with due decision make us know
What we shall say we have, and what we owe.
Thoughts speculative their unsure hopes relate,
But certain issue strokes must arbitrate; 20
Towards which advance the war.
[*Exeunt, marching*

ACT FIVE, scene 5

4 ague *fever*

5 forced . . . ours *reinforced with deserters from our side*

6 dareful *defiantly*
beard to beard *face to face*

7 home *decisively*

10 cooled *frozen*

11 fell *scalp*

12 dismal treatise *sinister tale*

13 As *As if. Compare I. 3. 135.*

14 Direness *Horror*

15 start *Compare III. 4. 62, and his resolution at the end of that scene.*

17 She . . . hereafter *She should have died later, at a less busy time – or, she would have died at some time or other. He does not even ask how she died.*

18 a time . . . word *an appropriate time for such news*

20 Creeps . . . day *One day creeps after another in the same trivial way*

21 recorded time *the record of time – or, the record of events made by the 'recording angel', who notes all our actions for Judgement Day*

22–4 all . . . shadow '*lighted fools*' *suggests the image of life as a candle flame, which in turn suggests the shadow of a person carrying the candle. There are echoes here of* Job, *viii. 9, xviii. 6, and* Eccelsiastes, *vi. 12.*

24 player *actor. The metaphor follows from* '*shadow*', *acting being only a shadow of reality. Compare II. 2. 53–5; now everything seems unreal.*

25 struts and frets *inadequately represents genuine dignity and anger. The imagery of the stage recalls the similar metaphor that Macbeth used when he was looking forward to being King (I. 3. 127–9) – he seems again to have subconsciously anticipated his later disillusionment. For an audience watching the players in a theatre, the whole play might suddenly seem to become a symbol of the unreality of his life.*

Scene 5. *Enter, with drum and colours,* MACBETH, SEYTON, *and* SOLDIERS

MACBETH Hang out our banners on the outward walls;
The cry is still 'They come'. Our castle's strength
Will laugh a siege to scorn. Here let them lie
Till famine and the ague eat them up.
Were they not forced with those that should be ours,
We might have met them dareful, beard to beard,
And beat them backward home.

[*A cry of women within*

What is that noise?

SEYTON It is the cry of women, my good lord. [*Exit*

MACBETH I have almost forgot the taste of fears.
The time has been my senses would have cooled 10
To hear a night-shriek, and my fell of hair
Would at a dismal treatise rouse and stir
As life were in't. I have supped full with horrors;
Direness, familiar to my slaughterous thoughts,
Cannot once start me.

Enter SEYTON

Wherefore was that cry?

SEYTON The Queen, my lord, is dead.

MACBETH She should have died hereafter;
There would have been a time for such a word.
Tomorrow, and tomorrow, and tomorrow,
Creeps in this petty pace from day to day, 20
To the last syllable of recorded time;
And all our yesterdays have lighted fools
The way to dusty death. Out, out, brief candle!
Life's but a walking shadow, a poor player
That struts and frets his hour upon the stage
And then is heard no more. It is a tale
Told by an idiot, full of sound and fury,
Signifying nothing.

31 should *would*
I say *I declare*

34 anon *at once*

40 cling *shrivel*
sooth *truth*
41 as much *the same*
42 pull . . . resolution *check my resolute course*
43 equivocation *See pp 1–2. Shakespeare uses the word in a more generally accepted sense than that adopted by Garnet. For him, to equivocate was merely to have mental reservations while telling lies, but the apparitions mislead Macbeth with ambiguous promises that in one sense are true – see V. 8. 20–2.*
44 That . . . truth *That deceives with the appearance of truth*
47 avouches *affirms*
48 There . . . here *There is no security in either. The prophecy contributes to Macbeth's downfall, since his desperation after its fulfilment drives him from the security of the castle (ll. 2–3).*
50 estate . . . world *structure of the universe*
51 wrack *wreck*
52 harness *armour*

ACT FIVE, scene 6

The orderly entrance of Malcolm's army to regular drum beats contrasts with the frantic confusion of Macbeth's directions to his forces.

2 show . . . are *appear like soldiers*
uncle *See note to V. 2. 2.*

Enter a MESSENGER

Thou comest to use thy tongue; thy story quickly.

MESSENGER Gracious my lord, 30

I should report that which I say I saw,

But know not how to do't.

MACBETH Well, say, sir.

MESSENGER As I did stand my watch upon the hill,

I looked toward Birnam, and anon methought

The wood began to move.

MACBETH Liar and slave!

MESSENGER Let me endure your wrath if't be not so.

Within this three mile may you see it coming;

I say, a moving grove.

MACBETH If thou speak'st false,

Upon the next tree shalt thou hang alive

Till famine cling thee. If thy speech be sooth, 40

I care not if thou dost for me as much.

I pull in resolution, and begin

To doubt th' equivocation of the fiend,

That lies like truth: 'Fear not, till Birnam wood

Do come to Dunsinane'; and now a wood

Comes toward Dunsinane. Arm, arm, and out!

If this which he avouches does appear,

There is nor flying hence, nor tarrying here.

I 'gin to be aweary of the sun,

And wish th' estate o' the world were now undone. 50

Ring the alarum bell! Blow wind, come wrack!

At least we'll die with harness on our back.

[*Exeunt*

Scene 6. *Enter, with drum and colours,* MALCOLM, SIWARD, MACDUFF, *and their Army, with boughs*

MALCOLM Now near enough; your leafy screens throw down,

And show like those you are. You, worthy uncle,

4 first battle *main force*

6 order *plan of battle*

7 power *army*

10 harbingers *heralds – see note to I. 4. 45*

ACT FIVE, scene 7

The 'alarums' that ended the last scene intensify, so that there is no break in the action.

1 a stake *The post to which a bear was tied when it was to be baited. The metaphor suggests his isolation – unlike Malcolm, he enters alone.*

2 course *bout with the dogs*
What's he *Who is he – or, what sort of a man is he*

11 prove the lie *prove it to be a lie*
[YOUNG . . . slain] *There is no opportunity for the body to be removed; as it is not seen by his father he may be killed on the inner stage, and his body concealed by the curtain that hung in front of it.*

Shall with my cousin, your right noble son,
Lead our first battle. Worthy Macduff and we
Shall take upon's what else remains to do,
According to our order.

SIWARD Fare you well.
Do we but find the tyrant's power tonight,
Let us be beaten, if we cannot fight.

MACDUFF Make all our trumpets speak; give them all breath,
Those clamorous harbingers of blood and death. 10

[Exeunt. Alarums

Scene 7. *Alarums. Enter* MACBETH

MACBETH They have tied me to a stake; I cannot fly,
But bear-like I must fight the course. What's he
That was not born of woman? Such a one
Am I to fear, or none.

Enter YOUNG SIWARD

YOUNG SIWARD What is thy name?

MACBETH Thou'lt be afraid to hear it.

YOUNG SIWARD No; though thou call'st thyself a hotter name
Than any is in hell.

MACBETH My name's Macbeth.

YOUNG SIWARD The devil himself could not pronounce a title
More hateful to mine ear.

MACBETH No, nor more fearful.

YOUNG SIWARD Thou liest, abhorred tyrant; with my sword 10
I'll prove the lie thou speak'st.

[They fight, and YOUNG SIWARD *is slain*

MACBETH Thou wast born of woman.
But swords I smile at, weapons laugh to scorn,
Brandished by man that's of a woman born.

[Exit

16 still *for ever*

17 kerns *See I. 2. 13. Macbeth, like the earlier rebels, has to rely on hired mercenaries.*

18 staves *spear shafts*

either . . . Macbeth '*I strike at' is understood from the previous line.*

20 undeeded *without having performed any deeds*

21 note *distinction*

22 bruited *proclaimed by the noise*

24 gently rendered *peaceably surrendered*

27 The day . . . yours *You have almost won the day.*

29 strike . . . us *fight by our side – or, possibly, deliberately miss us with their blows*

ACT FIVE, scene 8

1 play . . . fool *Roman generals considered it honourable to kill themselves to avoid capture when they were defeated*

2 lives *living enemies*

3 hell-hound *Perhaps more than a term of abuse – see note to IV. 3. 233.*

5–6 my . . . already *Is this a sign of remorse, or does he remember the prophecy of the first apparition?*

Alarums. Enter MACDUFF

MACDUFF That way the noise is. Tyrant, show thy face.
If thou be'st slain, and with no stroke of mine,
My wife and children's ghosts will haunt me still.
I cannot strike at wretched kerns, whose arms
Are hired to bear their staves; either thou, Macbeth,
Or else my sword with an unbattered edge
I sheath again undeeded. There thou shouldst be; 20
By this great clatter, one of greatest note
Seems bruited. Let me find him, fortune,
And more I beg not.

[*Exit. Alarums*

Enter MALCOLM *and* SIWARD

SIWARD This way, my lord; the castle's gently rendered.
The tyrant's people on both sides do fight;
The noble thanes do bravely in the war;
The day almost itself professes yours,
And little is to do.

MALCOLM We have met with foes
That strike beside us.

SIWARD Enter, sir, the castle.

[*Exeunt. Alarum*

Scene 8. *Enter* MACBETH

MACBETH Why should I play the Roman fool, and die
On mine own sword? Whiles I see lives, the gashes
Do better upon them.

Enter MACDUFF

MACDUFF Turn, hell-hound, turn!

MACBETH Of all men else I have avoided thee.
But get thee back, my soul is too much charged
With blood of thine already.

8 terms *words*
Thou . . . labour *You waste your energy. The fight would be laborious, with heavy broad-swords, and they would need to rest.*
9 intrenchant *invulnerable*
10 impress *make an impression on*
11 crests *helmets*
12 must not *is fated not to*
13 Despair *Despair of*
14 angel *evil angel*
still *always*
16 Untimely ripped *Prematurely delivered, by a caesarean operation.*
18 better . . . man *spirit*
19 juggling *deceiving*
20 palter *trifle*
in . . . sense *with words that can have two different meanings*
21–2 That . . . hope *That keep their promises according to the literal meaning of the words, but deceive us in the hopes that those words raise.*
24 gaze . . . time *spectacle of the age*
25 monsters *freaks, such as those exhibited at fairs*
26 Painted . . . pole *Painted on a sign hanging from a pole.*
underwrit *written underneath*

29 baited *See V. 7. 1–2.*

32 try the last *fight to the end*

34 [Exeunt . . . slain] *This is the stage direction in the Folio, perhaps to indicate a long and bitter combat, but the entry of Macduff in the next scene might be more dramatic if Macbeth were killed off-stage. At the Globe it would have been necessary to conceal the body in some way (see note to V. 7. 11 stage direction).*

MACDUFF I have no words;
My voice is in my sword, thou bloodier villain
Than terms can give thee out! [*They fight*

MACBETH Thou losest labour;
As easy mayst thou the intrenchant air
With thy keen sword impress as make me bleed. 10
Let fall thy blade on vulnerable crests;
I bear a charméd life, which must not yield
To one of woman born.

MACDUFF Despair thy charm;
And let the angel whom thou still hast served
Tell thee, Macduff was from his mother's womb
Untimely ripped.

MACBETH Accurséd be that tongue that tells me so,
For it hath cowed my better part of man.
And be these juggling fiends no more believed,
That palter with us in a double sense; 20
That keep the word of promise to our ear,
And break it to our hope. I'll not fight with thee.

MACDUFF Then yield thee, coward,
And live to be the show and gaze o' th' time.
We'll have thee, as our rarer monsters are,
Painted upon a pole, and underwrit,
'Here may you see the tyrant'.

MACBETH I will not yield
To kiss the ground before young Malcolm's feet,
And to be baited with the rabble's curse.
Though Birnam wood be come to Dunsinane, 30
And thou opposed, being of no woman born,
Yet I will try the last. Before my body
I throw my warlike shield: lay on, Macduff,
And damned be him that first cries 'Hold,
enough!' [*Exeunt, fighting.*

Alarums. Re-enter fighting, and MACBETH *is slain*

ACT FIVE, scene 9

[Retreat] *Trumpet call to signal the end of battle.*
[flourish] *ceremonial fanfare to announce the entrance of Malcolm.*

2 go off *be killed*
by . . . see *judging by those I see here*

5 paid . . . debt *given up his life*

7 The which . . . confirmed *No sooner had his valour confirmed this (i.e. that he was a man)*
8 unshrinking . . . fought *post where he fought without flinching*

10 your . . . sorrow *the degree to which you should mourn*

12 hurts before *wounds on the front of his body – proving that he was facing the enemy*

14 hairs *Perhaps with a pun on 'heirs', showing how calmly he takes his son's death.*
16 knell is knolled *funeral bell is tolled – i.e. that is all the mourning that is called for*

18 parted *with life*
score *debts – continuing the metaphor in l. 5*

20 stands *i.e. on the point of a spear*
21 time *age*
free *from both tyranny and guilt – compare the similar use of 'franchised' (II. 1. 28) and 'free' (III. 6. 36)*
22 pearl *nobles – like the circle of jewels round the crown*
23 That . . . minds *Who proclaim you king in their hearts, as I have already saluted you aloud*

Scene 9. *Retreat and flourish. Enter, with drum and colours,* MALCOLM, SIWARD, ROSS, THANES, *and* SOLDIERS

MALCOLM I would the friends we miss were safe arrived.
SIWARD Some must go off; and yet, by these I see,
So great a day as this is cheaply bought.
MALCOLM Macduff is missing, and your noble son.
ROSS Your son, my lord, has paid a soldier's debt.
He only lived but till he was a man,
The which no sooner had his prowess confirmed
In the unshrinking station where he fought,
But like a man he died.
SIWARD Then he is dead?
ROSS Ay, and brought off the field. Your cause of sorrow 10
Must not be measured by his worth, for then
It hath no end.
SIWARD Had he his hurts before?
ROSS Ay, on the front.
SIWARD Why then, God's soldier be he.
Had I as many sons as I have hairs,
I would not wish them to a fairer death.
And so his knell is knolled.
MALCOLM He's worth more sorrow,
And that I'll spend for him.
SIWARD He's worth no more.
They say he parted well and paid his score;
And so God be with him! Here comes newer comfort.

Re-enter MACDUFF, *with* MACBETH'S *head*

MACDUFF Hail, King! for so thou art. Behold, where stands 20
Th' usurper's cursèd head. The time is free.
I see thee compassed with thy kingdom's pearl,
That speak my salutation in their minds;
Whose voices I desire aloud with mine:
Hail, King of Scotland!

27 reckon . . . loves *pay my debts by rewarding the love that each of you has shown me*

28 even *equal in obligations to each other*

29–30 Henceforth . . . named *From Holinshed.*

31 would . . . time *should be established afresh with the new era*

33 watchful *suspicious*

34 Producing forth *Bringing out of hiding*
ministers *agents*

36 by . . . hands *by her own violent hands*

37–8 what . . . us *everything else that demands our attention*

38 Grace *God*

39 measure *due order. Malcolm's last speech stresses order, divine grace and natural growth.*

41 Scone *See note to II. 4. 31.*

ALL Hail, King of Scotland!

[*Flourish*

MALCOLM We shall not spend a large expense of time
Before we reckon with your several loves,
And make us even with you. My thanes and kinsmen,
Henceforth be earls, the first that ever Scotland
In such an honour named. What's more to do, 30
Which would be planted newly with the time –
As calling home our exiled friends abroad
That fled the snares of watchful tyranny,
Producing forth the cruel ministers
Of this dead butcher and his fiend-like queen,
Who, as 'tis thought, by self and violent hands
Took off her life – this, and what needful else
That calls upon us, by the grace of Grace,
We will perform in measure, time, and place.
So thanks to all at once, and to each one, 40
Whom we invite to see us crowned at Scone.

[*Flourish. Exeunt*